THE COMPLETE
BOXER

Tim Hutchings

RINGPRESS

Published by Ringpress Books Ltd,
PO Box 8, Lydney, Gloucestershire GL15 6YD

Discounts available for bulk orders.
Contact the Special Sales Manager at
the above address. Telephone 01594 563800

First Published 1998
© 1998 RINGPRESS BOOKS
& TIM HUTCHINGS

ISBN 1 86054 054 6

Printed and bound in Singapore
by Kyodo Printing Co

10 9 8 7 6 5 4 3 2 1

CONTENTS

This book is dedicated, with love, to two special sets of people and one particularly special Boxer:

● To Mum and Dad, Paul and Julie ... not forgetting baby Francis, who arrived in the middle of the project and provided a welcome distraction from the word-processor. My family have never shared my love of dogs, but they have always understood.

● To my partners in the Winuwuk Boxer kennel: Ivor, for a willingness to share his deep knowledge of the Boxer and for his belief in the importance of the next generation; Mims, for her unfailing kindness and the unbelievable affinity which she has with the animals in her care; and Julie, for her friendship, her competitiveness and her skill at presenting our Boxers in the show ring. I know that I would not be writing this book today, had it not been for the faith shown in Julie and myself by Mims and Ivor when they shared their dogs with us.

● To Misty, the Boxer of a lifetime.

ACKNOWLEDGEMENTS

Many people have helped me during this project, but none more so than my wonderful friends, Eddie and Helen Banks. Helen and Eddie were always asking after the book's progress and they provided so much practical help with photographs and proofreading. I could always rely on them, as honest, straightforward folk, to tell me what they really thought and their comments were immeasurably helpful and constructive. I was also very relieved to take Walker Miller up on his kind offer to read through the chapters with veterinary content. In the UK, we are fortunate to have such a practical, Boxer-owning vet. Of course, any errors which remain (despite my proofreaders' best endeavours to put me right) are of my own making.

In between slaving over various editions of *Boxer Quarterly*, Linda Carnaby worked hard to perfect the illustrations of the Standard.

Marcia Adams was so kind when she let me loose on her amazing collection of photographs at the 1997 American Boxer Club Nationals. I also thank the breeders and handlers who responded so promptly and willingly when I asked them for the loan of photographs.

Finally, I must thank Andrew Brace for the part he played in getting this book off the ground. I hope that he feels his confidence was well placed.

INTRODUCTION

I am a great fatalist. It is not far from Wycliffe College in Stonehouse to my family home in the small Gloucestershire village of Leonard Stanley, but, importantly, part of this short route used to take you left by the Ship Inn (now demolished to make way for a by-pass) and into Downton Road. When cycling along this road on the way home from school, I used to stop outside a cream-coloured bungalow where a puppy run looked straight out onto the street. There were often picture-perfect baby Boxers in this kennel and, in common with half the neighbourhood, I used to make friends with them through the wire. My parents have never owned a pet of any kind – never wanted to – so the lure of these Boxers was simply too much to resist.

During one Summer in the early 1980s, a couple of years before my O-levels, I plucked up the courage to write a letter to the owners, who had their names and address posted on a sign outside the front gate. I asked them whether it would be possible for me to walk their dogs and I made it clear that I was more than happy to dip into my pocket money and pay for the privilege! At the time, I thought that I was writing to a couple of dog lovers who just happened to own a lot of Boxers. I had absolutely no idea that these Winuwuk Boxers, owned by Marion and Ivor Ward-Davies, were world-class show dogs.

Anyway, I was soon walking the length

Ch. Winuwuk Jubilation.

The ideal companion.
Ashbey Photography.

and breadth of the Cotswolds accompanied by some very famous Boxers indeed. Looking back, I find it quite amazing that Marion and Ivor were so relaxed about seeing some of their best Champions and imports taken out by a young lad who had absolutely no experience of dogs whatsoever. Today, I am not at all sure that I would allow the same thing to happen, but this is the nature of the people – and they certainly never wanted my pocket money!

Throughout O-levels and A-levels, my interest in the Boxers became keener and keener and developed from the muck-shovel to the show ring. During the school holidays, Marion and I took the opportunity of virtually rebuilding the fabric of the kennels from top to bottom and then, in 1986, the 'modern' Winuwuk partnership was formed when Marion and Ivor shared their affix with Julie Brown and myself. Subsequently, my enthusiasm remained completely undimmed during the three years I spent at university in Oxford (when the number of shows I missed could

The inquisitive Boxer – Glenfall Finale.

be counted on the fingers of one hand) and, now that I am well into my working life, the Boxers and the Boxer scene are still my passion.

At the time of writing, in 1998, our puppy run no longer looks out onto Downton Road and passers-by can no longer stop to say hello. This is because we reluctantly had to block our kennels off to the outside world after a couple of unbelievable thefts. Our dogs are now surrounded by tight security, which is a sign of the times, I'm afraid. I am just eternally grateful that my schooldays were spent cycling past an open puppy run, or my life today might well have been very different indeed!

In the last couple of years, the Boxers have taken me all over the world from Australia to America, Scandinavia to South Africa, and it is always a pleasure to meet fellow enthusiasts. During these showing or judging trips, it is inevitable that we will all have our own slightly different appreciation of the finer points in the show ring, but we can always agree that our Boxers are the most wonderful companion dogs. For me, added to their striking good looks, it is their love of life and unfailing enthusiasm which are the breed's unique selling points. But the list of qualities is much more comprehensive than this and would include their intelligence, their inquisitiveness, their great love of children, their loyalty and their courage. Boxers have changed many people's lives for the better, including my own.

It is only when you start pulling a book together that you realise how many other breed books there are on the market. In writing this one, I have tried to maintain a slightly different focus. All the main topics are covered in detail, but within the text I have deliberately concentrated on those areas which I think benefit the most from individual interpretation and recent practical experiences. I have also made use of some up-to-date technical wizardry and I hope that readers will find the computerised images accompanying the section on the Breed Standard to be useful. *The Complete Boxer* is offered to its readers as a book with an unashamedly modern outlook. My relative youth has a few drawbacks, as some of my sterner critics will undoubtedly point out, but it does have the benefit that I have a much clearer recollection of doing things for the first time, and I hope that first-time owners or exhibitors will benefit from this.

1 ORIGINS AND DEVELOPMENT

The relationship between man and dog is an old one which stretches back many thousands of years to the time when the innate usefulness of dogs as hunters, guards or companions was recognised. There is certainly lots of evidence to suggest that for as long as man has used dogs, he has carried out an element of selective breeding in an attempt to equip them most accurately for the function they have to perform. Some dogs had to be racy and lean, built for speed, while others had to be squat and powerful, designed to latch on to bigger, slower-moving prey until hunters could arrive and finish off the quarry.

In the wooded landscape of Northern Europe where boars, bears, wild ox and the like were hunted, strong, brave, solid dogs were required, with the intelligence to avoid injury. These dogs were known as 'beissers' (literally meaning biters) and there were sub-types, denoted by their prey – such as the Barenbeisser (bear biter) and Bullenbeisser (bull biter). However, by the time that man had become less dependent on hunting, through the domestication of farm animals, these stocky dogs were increasingly used in sports such as bull-baiting in which the forebears of the English Bulldog were keen competitors. It is from these roots that the Boxer breed undoubtedly descends and, although bull-baiting was outlawed in the early 1800s, the type of big-hearted baiting dog which it had spawned remained popular in Europe.

THE BOXER IS BORN IN GERMANY
To establish the formal link with Boxer history, we need to move forward to the closing years of the 19th century, when a Munich man, George Alt, brought a brindle and white bitch of Bullenbeisser type back from France. She was called Flora and he mated her to a local dog of similar type. A puppy from the litter was bought by one of George's friends, Herr Lechner, and the dog was known as Lechner's Boxel. It is fairly obvious that a corruption of this led to the breed's name, but why Herr Lechner called his dog Boxel in the first place is not clear – maybe it is the name of a place or maybe he just made it up, though more probable is that Boxel was simply a common slang name used for this type of mixed breed.

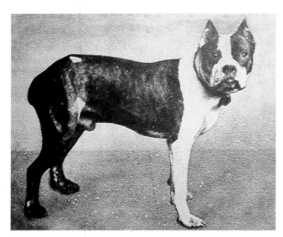

Muhlbauer's Flocki, the first registered Boxer.

In an early example of in-breeding, George put Flora back to her son and bred the check-marked bitch Alt's Scheken. At this stage, George obviously felt that he needed to bring some hybrid vigour into his line and, when it came to mating Scheken, he looked for an outcross. At the time, a Dr Toenniessen lived in Munich who owned an English Bulldog called Tom. George Alt thought that Tom would suit Scheken, the pair were mated and a litter was born on February 26th 1895, which contained Muhlbauer's Flocki.

Later in 1895 an Austrian, Friedrich Roberth, had come to Munich and, although he owned Bulldogs and Airedales, the new dogs being bred caught his eye. He teamed up with the local fanciers and persuaded the St Bernard Club to put on a Boxer class at their next show. Four Boxers turned up, including Flocki, who won and therefore became the first Boxer registered in the German Stud Book. The following January, the Deutscher Boxer Club was formed, and on March 29th 1896 it held its first show which had 20 entries.

The Flocki mating was repeated to produce Blanka von Argentor, then Lechner's Boxel was once again put to Flora to produce Maier's Lord who sired a white dog called Piccolo von Argentor. I am sorry for firing all these names at you, but it is important that we get to this point because Piccolo was eventually mated to Blanka and one of their puppies was Meta von der Passage, the real cornerstone of the breed. Meta produced a number of important Boxers, including Hugo von Pfalzgau and Ch. Giggerl. Hugo then sired Ch. Kurt von Pfalzgau. Line breeding on Meta, Kurt sired Ch. Rolf von Vogelsberg when mated to one of Giggerl's grand-daughters.

By now, Boxers had progressed a long way, but they were about to be taken to new heights by the real mother and father of the breed, Friederun and Philip Stockmann, whose von Dom kennels retain a legendary reputation the world over. Ch. Rolf von Vogelsberg was up for sale in 1911 and the Stockmanns, newly married, spent the 1,000 marks which they had earmarked for their house on buying him instead. Their faith was justified, for he became an outstanding winner and the foundation of their future breeding programme. One of his sons, Dampf von Dom, who was born in 1912, became the couple's first homebred Champion. He was also the first in a line of important von Dom Boxers exported to America. Indeed, Dampf became the first American Boxer Champion in 1915 for his owner, The Hon. Herbert Lehman, a keen breed enthusiast and one-time Governor of New York.

As war ripped through Europe, breeding activities were curtailed. Along with about 60 other Munich Boxers, Ch. Rolf von

Vogelsberg was called upon for war duties and Philip Stockmann was assigned to organise the military deployment of the dogs. One possible by-product of the war was the move away from white and check-marked Boxers, since war dogs with flashes of white made easy targets for snipers. Thankfully, Rolf returned from the war unscathed, and he took his final Championship after hostilities had ended, well into his eleventh year – a remarkable Boxer.

A few years later, the Stockmanns had one of Rolf's descendants, a striking fawn male called Sigurd, who had excelled in the show ring and as a stud dog. In May 1934, at the age of five, Sigurd was imported into America by Charles Ludwig, who immediately sold him on to Mrs Miriam Breed of the Barmere affix. Sigurd became a Best in Show winner and, although he was limited by the number of bitches available, he sired 16 US Champions before his death on March 3rd 1942.

THE BIG FOUR: SIGURD, DORIAN, LUSTIG AND UTZ

Sigurd was the first of what has become known in America as 'the Big Four' – a quartet of tremendously important dogs in the development of the US Boxer. The other three were all Sigurd grandsons and they are mentioned here in the order they arrived in America.

Dorian von Marienhof was purchased by Mr and Mrs Jack Wagner, whose Mazelaine kennel was to become so influential within the breed in America. Dorian reached the United States by boat on January 5th 1936 and had an outstanding show career. He was the first Boxer to win the Working Group at the famous Westminster Show

As well as being a great breeder, Friederun Stockmann was also a talented artist. This is one of her outstanding carvings.

and his grandson, Ch. Warlord of Mazelaine, was the first Boxer to go Best in Show there. A few years later, the Wagners' best Boxer, Ch. Mazelaine's Zazarac Brandy, was the second Westminster Best in Show winner for the breed, soon followed by the outstanding Ch. Bang Away of Sirrah Crest – also a descendant of Dorian and called 'little Lustig' by Frau Stockmann when she judged him as a baby puppy. A few years ago, I had the exceptional good fortune to see film footage of Warlord, Brandy and Bang Away being paraded together. It quite took my breath away. The influence of Dorian, who sired nearly 40 Champions in the first generation alone, was clear to see. Bang Away went on to become the most influential Boxer of all time with 121 Best in Shows All Breeds and 81 American

Int. Ch. Sigurd von Dom of Barmere.

Int. Ch. Lustig von Dom of Tulgey Wood.

Int. Ch. Dorian von Marienhof of Mazelaine pictured with his owner John Wagner (left) and another early pioneer of the Boxer in America, Valentine Martin.

Int. Ch. Utz von Dom of Mazelaine, pictured with John Wagner after taking Best of Breed at Chicago.

Champion children. Lustig von Dom was born on December 28th 1933, the result of a half-brother/half-sister mating. It took a long time for his nose to blacken in and so Friederun Stockmann hung on to him and soon began to realise how good he was. He quickly realised his potential in Germany and he attracted much attention, particularly from the United States because, ever since Sigurd had gone there, many wealthy Americans were in the market for the best German dogs. Eventually, at a time of great hardship in the Stockmanns' lives, an American agent offered them 12,000 marks for Lustig, and he was exported to Erwin Freund of the Tulgey Wood Kennels. He arrived in 1937 wearing a collar and name disc which simply stated: "I am the glorious Lustig". Glorious, indeed! He was never beaten in the breed ring, retiring in September 1938, aged five and a half, with 20 Best of Breeds from 20 shows. He then went on to sire 41 Champions. The description by Frau Stockmann in her wonderful book, *My Life With Boxers,* of the time when she visited her beloved Lustig's grave many years after his death is enough to bring a tear to anyone's eye.

For the fourth dog, we return to the Wagners who saw Utz von Dom in 1937 during a trip to Germany. He was bred identically to Lustig but from a later litter, and they attempted to purchase him there and then, but it was not until 1939, just

The three early Westminster Best in Show winners (left to right): Ch. Warlord of Mazelaine, Ch. Mazelaine's Zazarac Brandy and Ch. Bang Away of Sirrah Crest.

before the outbreak of war, that he arrived at the Mazelaine Kennels. He also became a Group winner at Westminster and sired 37 Champions – among them was Warlord who was bred out of a Dorian daughter.

This quality von Dom breeding, the combination of circumstances (from war to money) that made it available to the Americans, and the clever way in which breeders combined the lines of these four immortal males made sure that the American Boxer progressed in leaps and bounds and was usually a serious contender in the Group and Best in Show ring. This was the golden age for the breed and right at the forefront of this progression were some very famous names in addition to Mazelaine, Sirrah Crest and the like. Brayshaw, Canyonair, Cherokee Oaks, Eldic, Flintwood, Jered, Rainey-Lane's and Treceder all spring to mind. So does Grayarlin, the Boxer kennel established by that great professional handler Jane Forsyth, which in turn spawned the Hamilburgs' Salgray kennel whose name derives from their very first Boxer, *Sal*ly of *Gray*arlin.

The Salgray kennels have achieved huge successes over the years, helped by their famous 'F' litter, born when the Hamilburgs mated their Ch. Salgray's Battle Chief to the bitch which they had bought from Robert Burke, Ch. Marquam

Hill's Flamingo – a very good Best in Show winner. The litter of six contained four Best in Show winners: Ch. Salgray's Fashion Plate, Ch. Salgray's Flying High, Ch. Salgray's Flaming Ember and Ch. Salgray's Fanfare. Of these, Fashion Plate and Flying High became Sires of Merit with 90 Champions between them, and Flaming Ember was a Dam of Merit. Just in case you were wondering, the other two bitches in the litter also became Champions! Fashion Plate's influence was also very powerful in subsequent generations through his son and grandson, Ch. Millan's

Friederun Stockmann judging Ch. Bang Away of Sirrah Crest as a puppy.

Fashion Hint and Ch. Scher-Khoun's Shadrack, two more wonderful producers of outstanding Boxers.

THE EARLY YEARS IN BRITAIN

So far in this history lesson, you will have noticed that Germany and America have dominated proceedings, so what was happening in the UK? A bitch called Jondy seems to have been the first British Boxer in 1911. She was a grand-daughter of Meta von der Passage but was never bred from. Among the very early enthusiasts, Mrs Sprigge really got things moving by persuading Charles Cruft to schedule Boxer classes at his 1936 show. Later in the same year, Kitty Guthrie (a well-known Great Dane breeder under the Maspound affix, but with an interest in Boxers) started using her breed notes to whip up interest in a Boxer Club. Soon, the British Boxer Club was formed and Mrs Sprigge became its first secretary and treasurer.

A few Boxers were being imported at this time. Mrs Sprigge herself had a French dog and a Dutch bitch, and that famous dog man, Bill Siggers, imported a bitch from Munich who produced Cuckmere Krin, winner of the very first Boxer CC in the UK, awarded at the LKA show in 1939. The first Champion, made up later in that year, was Mrs Caro's Ch. Horsa of Leith Hill, who had been bred by Mrs Sprigge. Allon Dawson was another important name in these early years. He was a very wealthy individual, having made his money from the Northern textile industry, and he had a real interest in the breed. Among others, he imported a bitch in whelp to the great Lustig and this litter contained a couple of CC winners for his Stainburndorf kennels. Allon Dawson also bought the Lustig son

Ch. Panfield Tango, an important stud dog in the early years of the British Boxer.

Zuntfig von Dom, so the UK was beginning to get some of the renowned von Dom breeding, but the timing could not have been worse, as the Second World War was just around the corner.

As war raged, breeding and showing activities came to a standstill and Zuntfig von Dom was sold to America in order to raise funds for the British Red Cross. Although Allon Dawson brought in some more good dogs of von Dom breeding after the war, Zuntfig was a big loss. So, after a promising start in the 1930s, the British Boxer emerged considerably weaker after the war and, while the Americans were cracking on with the incomparable bloodlines provided by the 'Big Four', the UK was left playing 'catch up'.

A critical turning point in re-establishing the UK breed came when Elizabeth Somerfield, Marian Fairbrother and Mary Davis managed to buy Alma von der Frankenwarte, a Lustig daughter who was living in London as a pet. Of course, in subsequent years, Elizabeth Somerfield's Panfields and Marian Fairbrother's Gremlins were to become two of the country's most successful Boxer kennels ever. In time, Alma was mated to her own grandson to produce Ch. Panfield Serenade, the first bitch Champion in the UK, and her next litter contained Ch. Panfield Tango, who was such an important stud dog, producing four Champions before he was sold to Australia.

In 1946, when the war was over, Boxer shows resumed in style with the very first British Boxer Club Championship show, which was held in Coventry. The judge, so befitting of the occasion, was Jack Wagner of the famous Mazelaine kennels in America. Sadly, there are few people left in the UK today who remember this show, but those who do, including Millicent Ingram of the Tirkane Boxers, remember it as a real turning point, since Wagner was looking for elegance and style in his Boxers rather than the heavier, 'Bulldoggy' type. In his report, he gave UK breeders the lead they needed when he wrote: "My greatest disappointment was in the bulkiness I found almost throughout, wide fronts, heavy shoulders going back to quite light hindquarters...we have been fortunate in the USA to have such famous imports as Dorian, Utz, Lustig and Sigurd to use as patterns and try to improve upon...I feel that English breeders have to some degree lost sight of the fact that the Boxer is fundamentally a working dog, and such a dog must be able to jump and must be able to travel at top speed for great distances. Such a dog cannot be found in the Mastiff and the Bulldog."

In the years following the Wagner show, British breeders took heed of his advice and with the continued use of valuable imports from Continental Europe and America, the Boxer progressed quickly. George Jakeman, by somewhat dubious means had ended up with the lovely Dutch bitch Ch. Favorite

vom Haus Germania and one of her puppies who became Ch. Holger von Germania – a very important sire. Jakeman also had a hand in the arrival from Germany of Champus von der Fischerhutte, who sired the first Breakstones Champion for Hilary Gamble and Joan Dunkels. This partnership also imported two good sires from Holland, Breakstones Helios vom Haus Germania and Faust vom Haus Germania.

In the meantime, Marian Fairbrother had come by some good early German stock, and Gremlin Champions started to crop up regularly. One of the nicest, Ch. Gremlin Inxpot, was by Axel von Bad Oeyn, the German dog on lease to Dibbie Somerfield. Dibbie was also given Mazelaine's Texas Ranger by the Wagners. Texas Ranger was full brother to the great Ch. Bang Away of Sirrah Crest and he sired many classy Champions. Major Bostock also incorporated Mazelaine breeding when he bought the Bang Away daughter Beaulaines Bonadea, in whelp to Ch. Mazelaine's Gallantry. This was strong line-breeding on Utz and Dorian and it resulted in a couple of Burstall Champions.

Returning to Holger for a moment, he was only the fifth UK Boxer Champion, but his daughter, Ch. Orburn Kekeri, was the very first Boxer to go Best in Show All Breeds at a Championship Show which she did at Birmingham National in 1949. When you think back to Wagner's 1946 criticisms of the UK Boxers, and then look at the degree of elegance shown by Kekeri, it is clear how fast the breed had come on. Kekeri was owned by Nan Hullock, who mated her to the Dutch import Helios. This produced Ch. Winkinglight Viking, a major winner at the time who eventually went to

Ch. Orburn Kekeri, the first Boxer to go Best in Show at an all-breeds Championship Show in the UK.

Canada. Nan then linebred on Kekeri to produce Ch. Winkinglight Justice who sired seven Champions. The Winkinglights really provided the foundation upon which the subsequent success of the Wileys' Wardrobes kennel was built. As we will see, the Wardrobes Boxers were vital in UK Boxer history.

The Winkinglight breeding was also used to good effect by Pat Withers' Witherford Boxers who won many top awards, and the first Champions for Felicia Price's Felcign and Joan Maclaren's Braxburn kennels were also by Winkinglight stud dogs. I always think that the importance of Nan Hullock's Winkinglight Boxers is understated in the text books, perhaps partly due to Nan herself, whom I had the pleasure of meeting a few years back. We spent the afternoon talking about her life in dog breeding and I found her to be one of the most modest, kind and gentle people I had ever met. Seeing her on that afternoon, talking about her lovely Boxers while surrounded by four generations of her own family, is an

experience I will not forget. Peggy Haslam combined some useful American lines to come up with Ch. Geronimo Carissima who won 17 CCs. Then the Rainey-Lane's breeding from the USA came to the fore, firstly through the Bardens' Felmoor Rainey-Lane's Raffles who sired or lies behind Ch. Felcign Fiona (the second Boxer to go Best in Show All Breeds) and a couple of Pat Dellar's Merriveen Champions, including the very lovely Ch. Merriveen Fascination, a Crufts Best of Breed winner. Further lustre was then added to this famous affix when, in 1958, Marian Fairbrother imported Ch. Rainey-Lane's Sirrocco from Donald Starkweather. By this time Marian had gone into partnership with Martin Summers, a very wealthy City man who used to own Sale & Co, the merchant bank. This was just as well, because Sirrocco cost £2,000, which was an enormous sum in the 1950s and quite enough to buy a very sizeable house. 'Rocky', as he was known, was brought back to the Gremlin and Summerdale kennels which were located at Liss in Hampshire on a sprawling country estate called Clayton Court. It was here, and later at his new country seat of Upham House, near Aldbourne in Wiltshire, that Martin Summers used to host the annual British Boxer Club Championship shows, where he would also entertain all the exhibitors to a sumptuous lunch in lavish marquees. These occasions are remembered with much affection by everyone who was privileged to attend.

This was undoubtedly a very glamorous era in which to be showing Boxers, and the Summerdales would often go to shows on board Martin's plane which was based in Portsmouth. Martin Summers remains a vice-president of the British Boxer Club and, although his interest in pedigree dogs came to rather an abrupt end, during the time of his partnership with Marian there were many Champions and Sirrocco built up a formidable record as the most successful imported sire of all time, with 13 UK Champion progeny. This record still stands to this day and UK Boxer breeders must be grateful that Sirrocco arrived. We must also give Martin some credit for bringing us the famous book *Boxer Blarney* by Marian Fairbrother and Peggy Haslam, since he sent the pair of them away to a flat in Cannes to write it and paid for the first edition to be published. Peggy also lived at Summerdale for a while, looking after Martin's Great Dane interests.

I met Martin for the first time at his Bournemouth home in December 1994 and he more than lived up to his reputation. He was perfectly charming and free from any airs and graces. He clearly looked back at his time in the dog world with the greatest affection, and he had many interesting stories to tell. It was fascinating to hear him recount the story of one occasion when he entertained Jack and Mazie Wagner at Clayton Court and Marian Fairbrother, Dibbie and Stafford Somerfield, Kitty Guthrie and Felicia Price also came to dinner – oh, to have been a fly on the wall that evening!

By the 1950s, the breed was well and truly on the map in Britain, registrations were exceeding 5,000 per year and many new kennels were enjoying show ring successes, thanks to the hard work put in by post-war pioneers. June Grover made up a Sirrocco son to start off a good line of Ackendene Champions and Peggy Ingram's

Bockendons were up there with Lorna Greathead's Rytonways, Hazel Izett's Hazefields and Jean Heath's smart red Starmarks, along with many, many others, including lots of kennels who are still winning at the highest level in the 1990s show ring and who are covered in the chapter on the modern British Boxer.

IN CONCLUSION

When looking back at the 100-year history of the Boxer, I am always struck by the dominance of a few specific bloodlines in shaping the breed, and by the enormous amount of importing and exporting that went on between America, Germany and the United Kingdom. So many dedicated breeders were striving to achieve the blueprint as laid down in their Breed Standards which all demanded the same type of dog. As we have seen, the early German dogs won everything that there was to win in America and then American dogs came back to further the breed in Europe. It does disappoint me a little that, 100 years on, the free flow of Boxers between countries has tailed off, now that variations in national type have become so accentuated. I do not think that there is a single German dog that could now win in the American show ring, and the same has been proved in reverse. Perhaps when 21st-century transport makes the dog show ring truly international, all Boxer breeders will be forced into rediscovering the middle ground of true Boxer type. Maybe we all need to remember the breadth of outlook shown by Friederun Stockmann, that brilliant breeder and artist who taught us so much.

2 *THE BOXER PUPPY*

The decision to buy a puppy of any breed is not one to be made lightly, and a lot of honest forethought and preparation is required. If you have never owned a dog before it is easy to underestimate the upheaval that a new puppy will cause to your home life as you know it today.

BEFORE YOU BUY

There is no doubt that dogs can be a tie and, from the moment your puppy arrives, weekends away, holidays, working late at the office, entertaining visitors and the like will all require that little bit of extra planning. You will find that keeping the house tidy will immediately become more of an uphill struggle, certainly in the early days, and especially when the weather is being less than kind. There are also the extra expenses to consider, of which the initial purchase price is just one small element. Proper feeding costs money, vet's bills can soon mount up even for routine matters and the fees charged by good boarding kennels do not come cheap. In short, you must give very careful thought to your own personal circumstances before

you start looking for a dog, and you must ask yourself whether it is right for you to have one and whether the time is right. As an example, there is no point even thinking about ownership if the dog will have to be left on its own for a large part of the day. It would also be unfair to set about buying a puppy if a major household upheaval were imminent, perhaps if a baby is on the way or when a house move is on the horizon.

Once you are completely satisfied that you are going into dog ownership with your eyes open, you must then be happy that a Boxer is the breed for you. It is worth having a long think about this before you do anything about tracking down a suitable litter, if only for the good reason that the breeder selling your future puppy will want to be convinced that you have considered all the pitfalls before he is prepared to entrust one of his pups to you. Boxers are a boisterous breed, full of energy and thriving on human companionship and activity, both mental and physical. These attributes give responsibilities to you, the owner. Your Boxer will like nothing better than just being with you, so you should be prepared to include him whenever possible. He will need a sensible amount of walking and free-running exercise and he will need to be made a full part of your everyday family life – this all takes time. To my mind, the breed has no equal, but it would be silly to pretend that they are faultless. Their exuberance sometimes needs a firm hand to control, especially in adolescence, and they vary in their approach to other dogs. These are all factors which you need to consider.

It may seem strange to start a chapter on choosing a puppy by appearing to put people off the idea of owning a Boxer altogether. This is certainly not my intention since, for every possible pitfall associated with Boxer ownership, I can think of another ten good reasons for wanting to share my day-to-day life with the breed. However, I am talking from my own viewpoint and from my own personal circumstances. Thankfully, each of us is different and the message must be that, in making your initial decision to become a Boxer owner, you must be honest about yourself and fair to the dog.

Sadly for you, deciding to have a Boxer is only the beginning and you must now think about your precise requirements. Would it be more sensible for you to have a dog or a bitch? Do you have any colour preferences? You may think you would like to have a go at exhibiting your Boxer in the future, or it may be that all you ever want your Boxer to be is a companion to the rest of the family. Whatever you want, it is obviously sensible to have a clear idea of your requirements before you set out to look.

DOG OR BITCH?
As far as a companion goes, there is very little to choose between the sexes. As long as the males are not being used for stud

The male Boxer, illustrated here by the upstanding Ch. Thasrite Prince Charming, has a more robust appearance than the female. His musculation is more apparent and he has slightly heavier bone.

work, which can lead to a more dominant nature, my experience is that the temperament of the Boxer dog and bitch is remarkably similar, although I do have a feeling that adolescence in the male (say 12 to 18 months of age) is more difficult, and dogs are a little more wilful during this time than their female counterparts. It is also fair to say that males can be more confrontational with other dogs and, even if individual bitches are similarly disposed, at least they are easier to control because of their slighter build. On the other hand, you do have the complication with females that

The beautiful Ch. Tyegarth Gin 'n' Cin: Although females should never appear light, they are milder in overall appearance.

they come into season once every six to eight months and this requires a change in routine for a couple of weeks to ensure that a pack of male admirers does not come flocking to your bitch's door. However, I have to say that I have always viewed seasons as little more than minor nuisances in my own house dogs, where the amount of mess is easily managed and it only requires a small amount of common sense to avoid unplanned puppies by making sure that gates are kept shut and by exercising the bitch carefully during her cycle. So, for a companion, there is not much to choose between the sexes, which is well demonstrated by the fact that breed books are split 50:50 as to which is 'best'. If pushed, I would say that my personal preference was for a bitch, but the sweetest-natured house dog I ever had was, in fact, a male.

However, the decision on your puppy's sex is a different matter altogether if you are interested in showing, when a bitch is the only sensible choice. If you buy a show potential dog pup and he does not quite make the grade, you are stuck – whereas with a bitch you can always hope to breed something better in the next generation, if you can find the right male for her (and remember, you will be able to have a pretty free choice from some of the best-producing stud dogs in the country). A well-bred bitch of average looks is worth infinitely more to you than the lacklustre dog, who will just take up valuable kennel space as you attempt to found your winning line.

COLOUR AND MARKINGS

As you will see when we consider the Boxer Breed Standard later in the book, there are two recognised coat colours, fawn (usually known as red) and brindle, though there are many variations within these two basic types, ranging from a light fawn to a deer red and from brindle with a light fawn background to a rich dark brindling. The

COLOURS
Within the two accepted coat colours of fawn and brindle, there are many variations.

ABOVE: Fawn: Ch. Bellcrest Just Watch Me.

TOP RIGHT: Red: Ch. Kenbru Mollyhawk.
Photo: Simpson.

CENTRE: Light brindle: Ch. Norwatch Slightly Sozzled.
Photo: Banks.

BOTTOM RIGHT: Dark brindle: Ch. Walkon Skittles.

possible addition of white markings on the face, neck, feet and chest adds further variety. The colour of your companion puppy must surely be a matter of personal taste and you will have your own ideas as to which combination you find most attractive. However, it is probably worth looking at litters with a reasonably open mind. We find that many people have set their hearts on a red only to find, when looking at puppies and adults in the kennel, that they actually quite like the brindles too! Certainly, if you are after a show puppy, you should be 'colour blind'. You want the best puppy. This will be hard enough to find without having your possible number of options halved by strictly specifying colour.

As well as the reds and the brindles, most litters will also contain a few white (or largely white) puppies. This colour is not recognised by the Breed Standard and these puppies cannot be shown or bred from, but this is where the differences between whites and their coloured littermates end. Although a fully-grown white Boxer is certainly not as attractive cosmetically (something for you to consider before you fall for that charming puppy), they can make good pets. However, be warned, they are not 'rare' or 'special' in any way and, due to the fact that they cannot be used for breeding or showing, reputable breeders will only charge about a quarter the price for their whites as they do for coloureds. Indeed some breeders have their white puppies put down at birth since, in common with other white animals, there is a greater than average chance that they will be deaf.

SHOW PROSPECT OR COMPANION

If you have chosen well, the breeder will try his hardest to find a suitable puppy that will meet your requirements. If you have told the breeder that you have no desire to show, then you will probably not be buying a Boxer of show potential, though the pup will hopefully meet all your other needs in terms of temperament, fitness and character. You must remember this if, in the future, you change your mind. Most breeders guard their reputations most carefully so, if you do subsequently decide to have a go at showing, please have the courtesy to phone the breeder and ask his opinion first. It is just possible that your

dog, bought as a companion, will be good enough to show but, if not, it would be unfair on the breeder to start exhibiting with a dog he sold you, in good faith, solely as a companion. If you want a show prospect, you should ask for one.

FINDING A BREEDER

By far the easiest and most reliable way of finding a sound, healthy, well-reared companion puppy is via the extensive network of show kennels who dedicate a large part of their lives to breeding better Boxers. If you are not part of this circle it can sometimes seem difficult to track a suitable kennel down, but it really is quite straightforward. Just pick up the phone and contact the secretary. The secretary will have a good knowledge of all the breeders in his area and, through regular contact with members at club events and shows, he will probably know who has puppies available and he will be more than willing to put you in touch.

Even if the breeder you eventually contact does not currently have a litter, the chances are that they will know someone who has, probably sired by one of his own stud dogs or bred out of one of his bitches. You should not be put off if you seem to be passed around a little before you identify a suitable litter, since most kennels do not breed puppies on a large scale, and therefore personal recommendation is very common when it comes to puppy enquiries. Alternatively, you could phone your National Kennel Club direct, as they do keep registers of puppies currently available. You could also ook at the breeders' adverts in the two worldwide breed magazines, *Boxer Quarterly* and the *Boxer Review*.

SHOW PUPPIES

However, if you are looking for a puppy of show potential, you will need to do a little more research, and attending a few shows is essential. You will see the largest number of dogs at the Championship Shows in the UK or the Specialty shows in North America, and your local breed club secretary will be able to tell you when these are taking place. Go along and buy a catalogue, which will give you the breeding details of all the Boxers entered, together with the names, addresses and phone numbers of their owners. Take a seat by the ring and get a feel for which breeding lines and kennels you particularly fancy. It is also worthwhile making a particular mental note of those kennels which have sold winning stock to other owners. You will see from your catalogue that the Boxers bred by each different kennel will usually be identified by a unique 'affix' to their names. For example, all the Boxers bred in the UK by Mandy Laidlaw will have her 'Roamaro' affix at the start of their name. However, when Mrs Laidlaw sells her Boxers, the new owners will probably add their own affix to the end of the name. For example, the bitch which we bought from Mandy, called Scotch Mist, soon became Roamaro Scotch Mist of Winuwuk thus identifying Mandy as the breeder and our Winuwuk kennels as the owner.

Any kennel which you can see has sold winners to others must be worthy of a place on your shortlist of ones to approach. I certainly believe that, when searching for a show puppy, you are best advised to choose a kennel that is breeding winning stock itself. This does not necessarily mean approaching the top exhibitors of the day, but I would urge you to find a kennel which at least has a track record in breeding consistent, show-winning animals, and you should not let distance be a factor when making your decision. As I mentioned when talking about colour, show puppies are hard enough to find without limiting yourself unnecessarily. If you only consider kennels within a 50-mile radius of home, you are doing yourself no favours.

Once you have narrowed your choice down to a few kennels that you like the look of, go and introduce yourself to the owners at the show. Common sense tells you that it is best not to try and chat to an exhibitor just as they are about to enter the ring, so wait for a quiet moment, when you will find that most breeders are more than happy to show you their dogs and discuss Boxers. Tell them what you are looking for, ask for advice and listen to what they have to say. Of course, puppies of real show potential do not come along very often and most kennels will probably have a waiting list – this is a good sign – so tell the breeder that you are quite happy to wait until they do have a suitable puppy. You may like to ask about any litters they may have planned and when they think these puppies might be due.

It is so important when making this initial contact that you feel you have some rapport with the breeder and confidence in what you are being told. In the purchase of your new show puppy, you will be heavily reliant on the breeder's experience and knowledge. I have a similar problem when buying cars, knowing next to nothing about them myself, so I do need to feel as comfortable as I can with the salesman who is guiding me through the purchase. But thankfully this is not the motor trade, and you will find it a lot easier locating a genuinely helpful dog breeder than I do when trying to find the same qualities in my second-hand car salesman!

VISITING THE BREEDER

After you have spoken with your chosen breeder at a show, it is sensible to follow your enquiry up by letter or telephone to register firm interest and to make sure that you get your name on the waiting list. You may also ask to visit the Boxers at home. This will give you a good opportunity to assess temperament and to see the dogs that are no longer being shown, but who may be their best stud dogs or brood bitches. This type of visit will also give the breeder the opportunity to quiz you heavily about your suitability as a potential owner. After this, no kennel will mind the occasional phone call while you are waiting just to let them know that you are still keen and seeking an update on when a puppy may be due. Once a litter is born, whether you are seeking a show or a companion puppy, you will certainly not be allowed to see the litter until they are four or five weeks of age. Until then, the mother and babies need plenty of peace and freedom from possible external sources of infection.

When visiting, please do not treat it as a day out, since, although your chosen breeder will be delighted to show you the pups, keeping a number of dogs is a time-consuming business, so it is always appreciated if potential puppy buyers arrive on time, do not bring lots of onlookers along for the ride and do not expect to be entertained for hours. Although it is hard, you should also not ask to see the puppies too often, since young dogs do need lots of rest and you must remember that yours will only be one visit of many, especially if it is a large litter. Once you have chosen your puppy, you should not need more than one more visit prior to collection. I am sorry if this all sounds a little harsh, but these are just a few small tips to keep your puppy purchase running smoothly.

SELECTING YOUR COMPANION

When you get to see the litter, please do not be put off if you do not get a completely free choice. For a start, most breeders only have a litter when they are seeking their next potential show puppy, so unless you are very lucky the most promising pup or two in the litter will not be going anywhere! In other cases, earlier buyers may have beaten you to it, or had their name on the waiting list for longer. There is nothing sinister in any of this and 'runts' in correctly reared litters are so rare these days that, as far as a companion puppy is concerned, the differences between brothers and sisters are often little more than cosmetic variations. However, I do believe that you should always be able to see the whole litter together so that you know this to be the case. If some pups are already spoken for, so be it, but you should at least be able to see them.

It is always good to see the sire and dam as well, since if they are well-adjusted happy dogs, then there is every chance that your puppy will grow up to be the same. However, this is not always possible, especially with the sire, where there is every likelihood that he will be a stud dog from another kennel. In some rare cases, the dam may not be there either, as the litter may be out of a bitch that the kennels had placed on breeding terms and she may have returned to her owners, but, as a rule, if the pups are less than six weeks old the dam should still be around for you to see.

However, by far the most important thing to look out for when selecting your puppy is the general condition and cleanliness of the litter, the older dogs, and the kennel as a whole. In terms of the litter itself, it almost goes without saying that the puppies should be clean, with bright eyes and noses, clear coats and inquisitive natures. Boxers invariably make bold puppies, keen to investigate anyone and anything, though you will have to make some allowance initially for the one who has only just woken up – they do take a little time to get their bearings. What you want to see is the puppies coming out to meet you and playing happily with their littermates. Any departure from this is so unusual that it will be immediately apparent and the best advice must be to steer clear of the puppy who sticks religiously to his box. When choosing, feel free to pick the puppies up when they come out to greet you. They should be perfectly used to being handled and a fit, healthy puppy will feel sturdy and robust when you hold him.

In terms of other considerations, you should tactfully establish from the breeder whether he has his stock heart-tested for freedom from aortic stenosis and, if you are buying a dog puppy, both testicles should be apparent by the time you collect. Some breeders believe that an undescended testicle can cause problems in later life so, although firm evidence is a little light, such a puppy is probably best avoided. Tails are another matter but, in my opinion, as long as docking continues to be legal, you should certainly go for a docked puppy every time. The short tail is a characteristic of the Boxer and there is strong evidence from countries where docking has been

banned that tail injuries in our breed have quickly become a major problem. The puppies' dewclaws should also have been removed, as these really can prove to be a nuisance in later life. Thankfully, these matters will all have been dealt with if you have selected your breeder sensibly and, in short, if the establishment looks well managed and the dogs look well cared for and loved, then you will not be going far wrong. It is only a matter of common sense and, if you are uncomfortable at any point, make your excuses and try somewhere else.

SELECTING YOUR SHOW PROSPECT
The most important thing to say at the outset is that every breeding line seems to mature in a slightly different way. The person who best understands how a puppy from a litter is going to develop is the breeder and so, once again, you are going to have to place a lot of trust in him. Presuming that you have chosen well and the breeder actually has a few good winning dogs himself, then listen carefully to his advice which will be based on seeing many of your puppy's ancestors grow and develop over a number of years. This knowledge is invaluable when selecting from a litter. However, before you start looking at the finer points, you need to satisfy yourself on all the considerations relating to the selection of a companion puppy since the 'show' part is merely an extension to the basic model.

I tend to find that between seven and nine weeks of age is the best time to choose a show prospect since at this age the pups are very much like smaller versions of the finished product. Leave it much later and they will have probably started growing in odd directions. At the seven-week stage, the

THE OUTLINE

The puppies featured here are very promising indeed – all of them have lovely, typical outlines. Note how they are standing over their front legs. This indicates that all three benefit from good length of upper arm, coupled with correct slope of shoulder, and because of this, their necks flow neatly in at the withers. The quarters are well made, with good width of upper and lower thigh already evident, even at this young age – and the pups' feet look fine. We can also see good 'growth bumps' towards the base of the front legs indicating plenty of quality bone for the puppies to grow away from.

pups should be used to being set up on a table so that their potential can be assessed clearly. The outline will already be very clearly visible. I like to see a firm, level topline and good tail-set, with a definite 'bottom' behind the tail which is usually a sign that the quarters beneath are well-made. The forehand angulation will also be very evident at this age and this is one of those areas that will not change. If the puppy is short in upper arm and stuffy in

neck on day one, it will stay that way. The shoulders should be well-laid and narrow where they meet at the withers, and the front legs should be straight, with the elbows held neatly in to the body. If your puppy has the benefit of this good forehand, it will stand over its front legs and have a very evident forechest, and it will also, hopefully, be standing on small compact feet. All of this is very desirable.

When set up, your show pup should

THE HEAD
These are very good heads in the making.
Note the very good balance of skull to muzzle, the nice eye and the slight dome to the top of the skull. Do not be put off by ear size at this age since puppies usually grow into their ears.

present a smooth outline with each component part flowing neatly into the next. Have a look at the selection of illustrations on page 26. All of the puppies featured grew up to become good winners in the show ring and I have attempted to draw your attention to the areas where I feel they score most heavily. It is also very interesting to see how they compare so closely 'in miniature' to the lovely Boxer outlines that we consider in Chapter Six.

Although the basic construction is relatively easy to assess in your show prospect, heads are a different matter and it is here that the variety between breeding lines is most marked. In some, head shape is there from day one and the puppy just grows into it, whereas in others, if you see a head that looks finished too early, you can be sure that it will coarsen unacceptably as the puppy grows. However, there are some general rules. In profile, your puppy's head

DEVELOPMENT
Illustrated by Ch. Ashgate Able Seaman of Seefeld.

It is quite common for Boxers to grow in different directions at different ages. It is unusual for Boxers to maintain their balance throughout puppyhood so you should keep faith with your puppy if he goes through an 'ugly duckling' phase.

Ch. Ashgate Able Seaman of Seefeld at five months.

At seven months he looks a little longer.

At two years old, he has ended up as a very well balanced male.

should already have a very definite stop and a pronounced rise of skull and, when viewed from the front, the characteristic balance of skull to muzzle should also be very apparent. Note how the two puppies featured on the previous page have this essential feature. The ears may look large, but do not worry too much about this, since the puppy will soon grow into them. It is also good to see a slight dome to the head of the young puppy, as I have found that dogs lacking this as babies often grow too thick in skull, destroying the balance completely.

Once you have considered the head, take a look at the mouth, where it is width of jaw that you must be looking for. The baby teeth may not be precisely placed in the desired straight line but, as long as the width is there, you can be reasonably confident that the finished mouth and jaw will be acceptable. You must also bear in mind that on a baby puppy it is much more common to see the bite only very slightly undershot, since this will develop considerably with age. In this regard, it is worth mentioning that although a definite chin is essential to the finish of muzzle and the expression of an adult Boxer, a pup showing lots of chin at seven weeks will be in danger of becoming too undershot in later life and there is no quicker way for your dog's show career to end than to have him popping his teeth out in the ring.

Before we leave this subject, we must just consider further cosmetic features. Your show puppy should ideally have the benefit of well-defined coat colour with a good black mask and, although they are not required by the Standard, fashion currently dictates that show Boxers invariably have some white markings on the face, chest and feet. Lack of these markings (most importantly the absence of white socks) can make a dog look very common, which is something to be carefully avoided in a show dog. You should also be happy that the pup's eyes are dark in colour and, for preference, the third eyelids should be pigmented, since this does help to preserve the expression.

Selecting a puppy with show potential is no easy task, so take your time, listen to the advice you are given, and see the puppy set up and moving around on the floor. Study the finer points and details that we have discussed, but also consider the overall picture and go for a puppy that has a definite look of quality. Finally, there is a lot to be said for making sure that the first show bitch you buy is reasonably line-bred since this will give you a solid foundation on which to build in future generations. I cover line-breeding in greater depth in Chapter Nine.

COLLECTING YOUR BOXER

The age at which you will be allowed to collect your Boxer pup will probably vary, and it is partly dependent upon how well the litter has progressed. Every so often, breeders do get a litter which needs to stay with the dam a little longer than usual but, as a general guide, you can expect to pick your puppy up between seven and eight weeks of age. Alarm bells should certainly ring very loudly if you are asked to collect before six weeks, as this is far too early. As far as your own circumstances go, it is always best to try and collect your puppy so that he will join you at a time when nothing exceptional is happening at home and you can get straight into a routine that will not be broken for a while. If this means that

you have to ask the breeder to hang on to the pup for an extra week or two, you will find that most are only too happy to do this though, out of politeness, you could offer to make a small contribution towards the pup's keep during these additional days.

Before the arranged day of collection, have a brief chat with the breeder to find out what pet food you should stock. Make sure that you have a good supply and do not forget to buy some food and water bowls. At this stage you should also buy a comfortable bed for your puppy and a few toys to keep him amused. You will find that the extensive selection of pet accessories these days is truly mind-boggling, and often rather expensive, so it is usually best to start off with just a few of the essential items and then you can buy more once you have established your puppy's likes and dislikes.

When the big day finally dawns, make sure that you arrive at the breeder's premises at the arranged time; take a large cardboard box and blanket with you which the pup can sleep in on the way home, and take a few towels or some newspaper to clear up any 'accidents' the Boxer might have. Some water and a bowl is also a good idea just in case the pup wants a drink but, if it is likely to be hot, please arrange things so that the journey back with the dog can take place away from the heat of the day.

Although you will be itching to get your puppy home, there are some important pieces of paperwork to be dealt with first. When collecting your puppy you can expect to receive:
1) A receipt for the money you have paid, which will also outline any special conditions of the sale. Both you and the breeder should agree any terms and sign the receipt.

2) A copy of the pup's pedigree.

3) The Kennel Club registration document which the breeder should have signed, thus allowing you to transfer the dog into your own name.

4) A full feeding chart.

5) Details of when the puppy was last wormed and the breeder's recommendation as to when you should next visit the vet to have the puppy re-wormed and vaccinated. In addition, you often find these days that breeders will provide you at the time of purchase with a cover note that will give your pup six weeks of free insurance cover.

When you are collecting your puppy, do ask the breeder any final questions you might have, listen to any tips he has for you and make sure that he is happy for you to telephone at any time in the future if you have any unexpected problems. Finally, please do not make an unnecessary meal of the journey home. You will find that if you just get straight into your car, start the engine and get going, the puppy will very soon settle down and go to sleep.

AN OLDER BOXER

Every so often, when looking for a companion or a show puppy, you may find that you are offered an older Boxer. This can arise for a number of reasons: the breeder may have run a couple of dogs on from a litter and only now decided which one is best for the ring; a dog may have reached the end of its show career; or a top show kennel may simply find that it has too many dogs to show effectively. My own view is that there can be many benefits in taking on the older dog. If you are after a companion, then all the early hassle is out of the way: the dog is usually trained to a

reasonable level and will invariably adapt very quickly to a new environment. This is especially true if such dogs are leaving kennels to live indoors. They very soon realise which side their bread is buttered on! As far as a show dog goes, it can be a good route into the ring, for you can be sure that, if a show kennel has kept the dog for some time, he will at least be of good quality, well-bred and trained for the ring. Although the home kennel may have decided that the dog is not going to become a Champion, this does not mean that he will not give a new exhibitor plenty of fun in the ring. Most kennels, ourselves included, have many success stories to tell of letting older dogs go to new companion or show homes so, if you do get the opportunity of taking an older dog, consider it very carefully.

BOXER RESCUE

Another way of finding an older companion is by contacting one of the rescue services, and a list of names and addresses can be obtained from any breed club secretary. Many Boxers end up in rescue through no fault of their own, because of marriage break-up, death of owners and the like. In these circumstances, having a dog from the rescue service is akin to taking an older one from a breeder, with all the attendant benefits. However, some Boxers that come through are more problematic (usually due to the inadequacies of their former owners) and, although these cases and prospective new owners are always assessed most carefully by the rescue workers, this situation is probably best reserved for those who have owned the breed before.

Due to the immense adaptability of the

Boxer and the dedication of the rescue workers, I am delighted to say that the majority of cases work out very satisfactorily, but please do your research carefully and find out all you can about the dog you are considering taking on. Finally, do remember that Boxer rescue is not supposed to be an easy way of locating a cheap dog. It is amazing how many people still contact rescue expecting to find a well-trained, perfectly socialised young red and white Boxer bitch for next to no money! Needless to say, this is not the classic rescue case and, of course, with any Boxer you have from rescue, you will not be given any registration papers so you will not be able to show or breed from that animal, and you will be expected to make a sensible contribution to rescue funds.

PRICE

It is impossible to give a precise guide to the price you should pay for your puppy, as this varies enormously from country to country, and the laws of supply and demand also operate. For example, top-class show puppies are always going to be hard to come by, so they will obviously command a higher price. Breed fashions also tend to change, sometimes making reds more desirable than brindles, bitches more popular than dogs, and so on. However, you occasionally hear of such outrageous prices being charged that I must give some guidance. Your very best safeguard is to ask your local Breed Club secretary, when you start looking for a puppy, roughly how much you should expect to pay. You will find that most breeders in a particular area usually charge fairly similar prices and the club secretary will give you a sensible price range within which to work.

BREEDING TERMS

Occasionally, in your search for a bitch puppy, you may be faced with the possibility of breeding terms as a condition of sale. This is a formal arrangement whereby you agree with the breeder, at the time of purchase, that you will give them one or more puppies back from your bitch's future litters. Although this may not seem immediately attractive to you, there are some benefits: it is often the only way that you will get your hands on a truly promising bitch puppy; by definition, the breeder will guide you through your bitch's litter as he has a vested interest in the end result; and it will also mean that the initial price of your bitch puppy will be less than if you were buying her outright.

On the other hand, it can be a little soul-destroying to raise a promising litter only to see the best puppy go somewhere else, though you must remember that you will be recorded as the breeder and this can only do your early reputation some good if the pup should go on to achieve success in the ring. It is also impossible for you to sell the rest of the litter before the owner of the pick has made his mind up, which can delay things and, if you are really unlucky and your bitch only has one puppy, it makes no difference and you must still let it go.

I personally believe that there are occasions when breeding terms are entirely appropriate and can work to everyone's advantage. The most important thing is to make sure that everything is written down and agreed at the outset, since this form of sale must be one of the primary causes of misunderstanding and unpleasantness in the dog breeding game. Be crystal clear. How many puppies are to be returned and from which litter? Who is going to choose the stud dog? Who is to pay the stud fee? Who is going to whelp the bitch? What if the puppies turn out to be white? And do be careful of terms which are too onerous – I would certainly think long and hard before I agreed to a commitment which involved more than two puppies.

SUMMARY

There can never be absolute guarantees with animals and, despite all your best research and the best endeavours of the breeders, not everything will always turn out exactly as you might have planned. For example, your show potential puppy may not end up quite as promising as you had hoped for, or your dog may unfortunately take ill at an early age, just like humans sometimes do. All dog owners have these occasional disappointments and they are a feature of everyday life with living creatures. If you have chosen well, the dedication of your pup's breeder will have improved your chances of success enormously, but dog ownership always involves some risk. We must always bear this in mind, even in today's 'sue and counter-sue' society, where misfortunes always have to be someone else's fault.

CARING FOR YOUR PUPPY

Nothing can alter the fact that leaving for a new home will be a traumatic time for a baby puppy. He has grown used to his surroundings, he has always had his littermates for company and all of this is now going to change abruptly – you are going to be all that the puppy has now got and, no matter how good-looking you are, you are bound to seem very big and very strange to an eight-week-old baby Boxer!

We have already mentioned some of the equipment you had to buy before you collected your new dog but, in addition to this, you must also have reserved a special place for him where you will have located his bed. Most people decide that the kitchen or utility room are the most sensible places but, wherever it is, it must be draught-free and warm. If you have the space, it also makes a lot of sense to surround his bed with a playpen because this will give you more control over him during the early weeks when he is settling in. From the moment you get the puppy home, you should have just one thought on your mind – and that is to start as you mean to go on. For example, if there are certain places in the house or garden that you have decided will be out of bounds, stick to them and be consistent.

When your puppy first arrives, try not to make a big deal out of it and carry on with your normal routine because, in the long run, this is what the puppy has to fit in with. You should not force him into new places and situations. He should be allowed to find his bearings at his own pace. Boxers are naturally a very inquisitive breed and it will not take him long to get his nose into most things, but it is probably sensible to limit him to just one room at a time, building up to all accessible parts of the house and garden. Each location will have something else for him to get used to, from the washing machine to the television.

The first night is always going to be difficult, but your pup must be made to sleep where his long-term bed is going to be – there is no point thinking that you can have him in your bedroom only for the first week or so. The most sensible course of action, just before you retire for the night, is to put a covered hot-water bottle in his

*ABOVE: Boxers are naturally inquisitive, and they will soon have their noses into most things.
Photo: Rummer Run Boxers.*

*LEFT: A new home is going to look very strange to an eight-week-old Boxer puppy.
Photo: Rummer Run Boxers.*

box, together with a loudly ticking alarm clock, firmly wrapped in soft material. These two items replicate, in some measure, the sensations of sleeping with littermates and they do help. You should also make sure that there is nothing at puppy level which is likely to do him an injury – or test your patience if you find it destroyed the following morning. Ideally, he should be placed in his pen. Once you have left the puppy, do not have second thoughts. He is bound to cry a little, but he has had a tiring day and very soon he should settle down and drop off. You will find each subsequent night easier than the first. One final precaution is to make sure that your heating is set so that the puppy's sleeping accommodation is never allowed to go cold.

ESTABLISHING A ROUTINE
During the daytime, do try and get into a routine of play, feeding and sleep which suits you. It is especially important that the puppy has long, undisturbed rest periods, and any children you have must understand this. Again, his playpen will come into its own. With a baby puppy, you will notice that everything is done in fits and starts with frenzies of activity being immediately followed by total crash-outs. You will also quickly realise that accommodating a new puppy into your home and into your own way of life is not done without a bit of damage, a bit of mess and a lot of patience. Having said that, compared to some breeds, Boxers do learn quickly and if you are lucky enough to have another adult dog in the house already, you will find that the whole process is made that much easier still.

FEEDING

Firstly, you must make sure that your puppy has access to fresh drinking water at all times. As far as feeding goes, you should take the advice of the breeder and follow the feeding chart which you were given. Our own method for feeding puppies is given in Chapter Ten and basically entails two milk-based and two meat-based meals per day until the pups are four months old. We then gradually cut out the milk meals until, by the time the pups are six months old, they are on just two main meat meals per day. However, we continue to give fresh cow's milk, straight from the bottle, for as long as the dogs will take it. We believe that this makes for good bone.

In terms of quantities, you have to put the goodness into Boxers as puppies or you will never get it into them. This means using good-quality food and keeping the puppies well-covered and prospering. Feeding a puppy is quite an art, and you will need to watch his condition most carefully to ensure that you are giving him enough. At a young age, a bit of puppy fat is far preferable to ribs and pin-bones on view. We also like to add a multivitamin supplement to our puppies' meals in the prescribed quantity, just to be on the safe side. In the past, we have suffered the occasional case of skeletal scurvy, but keeping Vitamin C intake up in puppies seems quite effective in avoiding this.

You may be concerned that, for the first couple of days in his new home, your puppy may be a little reluctant to polish off his rations. This is to be expected, if only for the reason that he no longer has to eat against the competition of his littermates. Do not be tempted to leave his food down for too long – you do not want to

Feed a good-quality diet, and keep a close check on your puppy's overall condition.
Photo: Carol Ann Johnson.

encourage a fussy eater. You will find that missing out once or twice will focus his mind next time, and this phase is normally very short-lived. You will also find it useful to feed him when there are no other obvious distractions, so that he can concentrate on the job in hand.

TOYS

Your Boxer puppy will need toys to play with and even the simplest things will do. Old plastic cartons and small cardboard boxes are particular favourites. It is also sensible to include the excellent sturdy

Your puppy will appreciate some toys to play with.

Photo: Carol Ann Johnson.

rubber toys that you can buy these days, since these will ease him through the teething process when you will welcome anything that diverts his attention from the legs of your tables and chairs. This chewing period usually only lasts until about five months when your pup's second teeth will have come through fully. Until they have, he will have razor-sharp needles for teeth and he needs to be taught at an early age that games with you that involve too much chewing are simply not on.

INOCULATIONS
The science of inoculations changes regularly and it varies enormously from country to country. At present, in the UK, we have our puppies jabbed by the vet at 10 and 12 weeks to give protection from distemper, hardpad, leptospirosis, hepatitis and parvovirus. Until your puppy has been fully inoculated, he should never be allowed off your property and he should not be

allowed to meet any strange dogs. A little later, we also have ours protected against kennel cough. Although this is not 100 per cent effective, it does seem to ensure that, even if they do pick up this nasty bug, it does not seem to take hold quite as badly if they have had some form of preventative therapy. It is most important that you have these inoculations boosted by your vet every 12 months. Some people will try and convince you that boosters are not required, but common sense tells me that it is better to be safe than sorry. The inoculations are protecting your dog from conditions which are particularly unpleasant, and you should not risk his contracting them for the sake of a few pounds.

ROUTINE HEALTH CARE
When you collected your puppy at eight weeks, the breeder will have had him fully wormed up to that date and it is important that you continue with this. As vets seem to

vary quite a bit in their approach to worming, we always recommend buyers to seek their own vet's advice when they have the puppy vaccinated for the first time at 10 weeks, since the dog will need worming again at this age. This first trip to the vet is also a good opportunity to get the pup fully checked over.

You should keep a close eye on the pup's nails and should trim them back if necessary. The other thing worth mentioning is the fact that you might be faced with an upset stomach now and again, especially when the puppy is first settling in with you and getting used to a slightly different diet. We usually find that a day of boiled rice and chicken settles things back down again, but do not hesitate to contact your vet if the problem continues.

EXERCISE

I often think that this is the one area which new owners of Boxer puppies generally get more wrong than anything else! While puppies are growing up, they actually need very little formal exercise indeed and, when they are youngsters, too much exercise is far, far worse than none at all. You will need to do a small amount of walking to get the pup used to the lead (as we shall see in the

Keep the nails in trim using the guillotine type of nail-clippers.

next chapter), but he certainly does not need to go out for long walks. By and large, puppies should be left at home to grow and they will get all the exercise they need from half an hour's play in their own back gardens.

Often, if there is a keen walker in their new family, you see puppies being dragged up hill and down dale almost immediately after their inoculations are complete. If you do this with a Boxer puppy, he will soon be doing a very passable impersonation of a Whippet, retaining no body condition or bone at all. Although we take our puppies out on the lead regularly for brief periods of training and socialisation, we certainly do not think about taking them on 'proper' walks until they are 10 to 12 months of age.

CRATES

A crate is a rectangular enclosure made of wire, with a top and a door. Crates come in a variety of sizes and their purpose is to provide guaranteed confinement of a dog for reasons of safety and general control. It has been a standard piece of equipment for dog breeders and exhibitors for many years, but individual pet owners often reject the idea as cruel to the dog.

I strongly believe that if crates are used properly they can have great merits: they allow you to leave your dog at home for short periods with complete peace of mind; they can effectively confine your dog at times when he may get underfoot or over-excited; and they can be a useful aid to house-training. As far as the dog goes, he can enjoy the privacy of a 'den', and I have yet to meet a Boxer who minds going into his crate for a short while.

Whenever we sell a puppy, we ask that the

A crate can be a very useful piece of equipment.

new owners give serious consideration to buying a crate and when they see how happy our own dogs are about using them, they tend to feel a lot more comfortable with the idea. However, there are two critical points to remember: firstly, you must get the dogs used to them from a very early age; and secondly, you must never over-use them – crates should only ever be used for short-term confinement.

EARS
Occasionally (usually as they start to teethe), Boxer puppies will 'fly' their ears. This basically means that the folds which normally make the ears hang neatly forward become a little erratic and lazy. As a result, the ears can look scraggy and untidy. This will probably only be a passing phase, but if it does start to happen with your puppy, take every opportunity to massage the ears gently back into the proper position, especially when the pup is resting.

It is unlikely to be needed, but if this slight problem persists, you can take a small piece of sticking plaster and tape the ear's main central fold in place for a while. This always does the trick. Although flying ears are obviously not a matter of life and death, they do tend to detract from the Boxer's characteristically noble and intelligent expression, so you are best off without them.

One ear hanging correctly and one ear 'flying'.

Photo: Banks.

3 TRAINING YOUR BOXER

Dogs in general and Boxers in particular are, by nature, very clean animals and your task in house training is simply to channel this natural instinct. From almost as soon as he is up on his feet, your puppy will have learned not to dirty his nest and, by the time you collect him, the chances are that he will already be used to using newspaper, placed at some distance from his box.

Every time your pup wakes up and after every meal, you should immediately take him to the same spot outside and wait for him to do his business. When he performs (it will not take long!), praise him lavishly. You should also pop him out whenever you notice him acting suspiciously inside. This is unmistakable when he starts taking lots of short little steps and begins 'circling'. Puppies feel the call of nature frequently and urgently, so you will need to be quick. If you have several ways out into the garden, I always think that it is best to take the puppy out of the same door every time you expect him to perform since, as he gets older, he will soon learn to 'ask' to go out of this door when he needs to.

You might be lucky, but it is a bit much to

expect a baby puppy to go through the night without spending a penny. Put a few sheets of newspaper right by the door and he will naturally use this until his bladder control improves with age.

During house training, there is bound to be the odd accident. If you do happen to catch the puppy at it, scold him sharply with your voice and take him straight outside to your preferred location. If you only notice after the event, there is absolutely no point shouting at the puppy – he will certainly not associate your anger with his offending action, no matter how recent it was. The 'traditional' technique of rubbing the puppy's nose in it has long been discredited and it is nothing short of barbaric. Clear up the mess immediately with disinfectant – you do not want any lingering smell to encourage the puppy to use the same spot again – and, by treating the area with a little soda in water, you will prevent any stain.

You will be amazed how quickly your puppy cottons on to the idea of needing to go outside and, from all the various breeds we have owned, I can safely say that Boxers are the easiest to house-train. It is also sensible at this early age to use the command "Be clean" when your puppy is performing. This will help you later on in life when, for reasons such as pouring rain or lack of time, you want a quick result when taking your dog out.

CAR TRAINING

There are few Boxers who do not end up loving a trip in the car, but their first experience is naturally going to be a bit daunting. When you are getting your puppy used to the car, it is much better if he is not rattling around in a lot of space – this is a recipe for sickness. Also, from a safety point of view, an unrestrained dog is as unwise as an unsecured child. In this respect, crates can be a great help, not only because they keep the dog still when he is travelling, but also because the crate will feel familiar and safe to him during this new experience. If you feel like splashing out, the cages specifically tailored to your make and model of car are absolutely ideal.

You should make your puppy's first car journey short and sweet. He should not have been fed for a couple of hours beforehand and you should stick to straight

A specially fitted car cage can be a great asset.

roads. However, even with these precautions, it is not unusual for a dog to be sick or make a mess during his first outing, so be prepared. After this, journeys can be built up gradually and you will very soon find that the dog settles down and goes to sleep almost as soon as you start the engine. We tend to find with our dogs that they are sick during their first long trip to a show, but never again. However, if you are unlucky and have a bad traveller, half a children's travel-sickness pill on a couple of occasions gets them out of the habit of being ill, and blocking off the rear side-windows can also work wonders.

LEAD TRAINING

You should start lead training your puppy at about ten weeks. He will not have completed his inoculations at this age, so your initial training must be limited to the confines of your property. To start with, we use a soft semi-choker, which is adjustable. You need to make it small enough to give some control and tight enough not to let the puppy slip out, but big enough not to choke him when he pulls away. Start off by putting this lead on your pup, then pick him up and carry him down the garden, away from the house. When you eventually put him down, you will hopefully find that he starts off in the direction of home quite happily with you walking beside him and without really realising what is happening. This is a good start, though at some point it will undoubtedly dawn on him that he is 'attached' and he may thrash around like a fish on a line. Calm him down and set off again.

If he ever sits down stolidly and refuses to move, do not be tempted to yank him about, just crouch down in front of him

The correct way to fit a choke chain with the dog walking on your left-hand side. Note how the chain will loosen when the dog is not pulling.   *Photo: Banks.*

The incorrect way to fit a choke chain with the dog walking on your left-hand side. If it is fitted like this, the chain cannot naturally loosen when the dog is not pulling
Photo: Banks.

and he will, normally, come running. Once you have made it back to the house, that is lesson one over. On subsequent days, repeat the same procedure and you will find that he quickly becomes used to the lead. When you are starting him off, you should let him go in whichever direction takes his fancy but, after a few days, you will find that he is quite happy to be led wherever you want to go.

When he is inoculated and fully comfortable with the basic idea of the lead, you can start to take him on short road walks but, for his first time out into the big wide world, you might find that, again, you need to start off by carrying him away from home and getting him to walk back. You will find that this is another area of training which your Boxer takes to easily and, within no time at all, he will positively look forward to going out.

While you are getting your pup used to the lead in the first place you must also break him of any inclination to pull, because Boxers can be great pullers if they are not checked. From the start, he must understand the command "Heel" and, during all your early walks, a semi-choker to bring him in line, a very firm voice and (most importantly) perseverance should bring results. From about six months, we move away from semi-chokers and start using full choke chains to walk our dogs. We find them excellent, but please do remember to fit them so that the loose end drops away and releases the pressure when the dog is not straining.

Of course, whether your dog wears one all of the time or not, you must ensure that he has a properly fitting collar and means of identification whenever you take him out, just in case you become separated.

SOCIALISATION

It is most important that your puppy is properly socialised. In simple terms, this means exposing him to a lot of different situations, people and animals from an early age so that he ends up as a well-adjusted member of the canine race who is not easily fazed. The breeder will have started this process and you must keep it up.

Before he can go out, your pup will have a lot of new and unusual things to get used to in the home and he must also be allowed to meet any visitors. When he can go out, your lead training and car training sessions are good times to combine with socialisation: walk the puppy along the road, through the playing field, through the village or down the high street. In fact, we find that one of the best places is the supermarket carpark – there is always so much hustle and bustle and you are never short of friends when you have a young Boxer on the end of a lead! The other invaluable place for socialising is the dog training class or the show training nights that will be run in your area.

LIVING WITH OTHER ANIMALS

We are often asked by prospective owners how a new Boxer puppy will settle into a house where there are one or two animals already in residence. The short answer is that, if you start off with a young pup, there are rarely any difficulties integrating him with the family's other pets. You need to respect the feelings of your current pets and you need to make sure that the puppy quickly gets to know what is not acceptable – such as chasing your cat – but animals have this habit of quickly working out a pecking order and, once it is established, you should have few problems.

This adult Boxer is quite happy to share the paddock with a Shetland pony.

BASIC OBEDIENCE

You have already dealt with quite a lot of this, since you have a Boxer who is clean in the house, quite happy in the car, and walking sensibly on a lead and who can be left on his own for short periods. What else should you be teaching him?

He must, of course, be taught to come back when he is called. I love seeing an adult Boxer running free, but, before you can risk it, you must first be happy that he will return at your command. One of the best ways of doing this is by channelling, at a young age, the natural insecurity of a puppy who will not want to be far from your side when he is away from home. On some of your early walks, let the puppy off the lead in an enclosed space. He will have a little sniff around and an investigation, but he will not go far. When he has been off for a short while, crouch down and call him

Keep training sessions short, and always end them on a note of success.
Photo: Carol Ann Johnson.

back by name. If things go true to form, he should come running immediately. When he reaches you, praise him generously. By conditioning this routine into him as a puppy, you should have few difficulties when he is older. However, if you do ever have problems getting older Boxers back, do not be tempted to chase after them, as they will think this is the greatest game ever invented and run you off your feet. The best bet is to make them feel left out, since a Boxer never likes to be away from the action. Call your dog's name and start walking quickly in the opposite direction. It will not be long before he comes running and, no matter how much it goes against

the grain, you must reward him for coming back. If you chastise him when he returns, he will not exactly want to come running to you next time, will he?

Jumping up is another habit that you should break early on. Boxers love jumping up and, while it might seem funny and just plain sociable in a puppy, it is not so amusing in a 60lb adult! With a youngster, the best way to deter him is with a gently placed knee to push him off balance. He will soon get the message that leaping up to say hello is not on. Some owners also find it useful to teach a dog to sit. This is not a difficult task and the straightforward command "Sit", together with pressure on the dog's rear, usually produces the desired result first time round. After several attempts, the dog will get the message without needing to be encouraged into position. However, if you want to show your dog, you must never, repeat never, teach him to sit before he has learnt to stand properly.

If you want to take your obedience training further or feel that you need some help with it, you can always join a local dog training club where formal lessons are held for beginners upwards, but it really does not take much effort or genius to bring a dog up to a reasonable standard of manners. Common sense tells you to be consistent, finish any training session with a success, only carry out training with your dog when you are in a good mood, keep the commands simple, do it little and often, reward with praise, and use the sound of your voice to indicate right and wrong. You should not need to resort to smacking a puppy, though I do think that most dog books are far too politically correct on this point. Personally, I do not believe that an

If your Boxers are well-socialised, they will earn many friends for the breed. Diane Mallett is justly proud of her well-mannered team.

Photo: Marcia.

occasional tap does any Boxer lasting psychological damage, and it can sometimes be very useful in focusing their attention when they have done something seriously wrong.

In addition to the basic elements of obedience, I also think that it is sensible to get your adaptable youngster used to any other things that he will have to experience at some time in his life. The obvious example is that of boarding kennels. If you are going to need to board your dog in the future, there is a lot to be said for putting him there for a few odd days as a puppy, so that it does not come as too much of a surprise when he is grown up. It is amazing how effective this can be.

SHOW TRAINING

Training for the show ring is not 'instead' of anything that I have described so far – it is

an addition to it and should be carried out from a very early age if you want to exhibit your dog.

Although you will not have picked up your puppy until he was eight weeks of age, his show training will probably have started a couple of weeks earlier when the breeder began stacking the puppies to assess their quality and conformation, so hopefully your puppy will already have some idea of what is required. It is very important that the young pup is comfortable being set up and that he gets used to your touch. For this early training, you need a small rubber mat placed on a suitable table. Pick the puppy up and rock him in your arms for a few seconds. The slight disorientation which results will make him stand solidly when he gets his feet on the firm surface. Place the pup on the table, then briefly lift all four feet again with your fingers under

BASIC SHOW POSE

Ch. Norwatch Glory Boy of Rayfos in basic show pose.   *Photo: Holley.*

Julie Brown is baiting Ch. Winuwuk Heaven Forbid with a small piece of cooked liver. Note how Julie still keeps the lead around her hand for full control.

the neck, just behind the ears, and with your other hand between the back legs. In one smooth motion, drop the front legs into position, followed by the back feet. If this has worked, your puppy will be in show pose. Throw something in front of him which should catch his attention, make him arch his neck and 'use himself'. Your fingers should still be supporting him beneath the neck while, with your other hand, you lift the pup's tail. Perfect!

The puppy should give no resistance during this exercise, and there should be no real pressure on your hands when you have him stacked up. Needless to say, this will all need a bit of practice. The one mistake you should not make is to handle the puppy as if he is made of fine china. Puppies like firm hands. When you have him set up, it is a good idea to have a look in his mouth and, if some of your doggy friends call, get them to 'go over' the puppy for you while he is on the table. You should set your puppy up in this way maybe once or twice a week.

By the time he is walking on a lead he will be too big for the table, and so you should start using his lead training sessions to get him used to being set up on the floor. After you have taken him for his short walk, spend a few moments stacking him when you return. While holding him with one hand firmly under the chin, put your other hand under his chest and drop his front into position. Then place each back leg individually by picking it up at the hock and setting it back down. To finish things off, just put your hand between his back legs and lift slightly upwards to make sure he has not 'sagged' in the process. Having done this, you have the makings of a well-presented show dog. As with other basic training, do this little and often and always end on a positive note. You should also remember that you will find your puppy easier to set up at different stages of his development because, at some points, he will be a little unbalanced and, for example, his quarters may not always set up exactly as you would wish.

The quick and easy method described above will get your Boxer into a basic show pose, but it is most essential that the breed should 'use itself' in the ring. This means that it is desirable for your Boxer to be arching his neck and looking alert. Some Boxers do this quite naturally and have an interest in everything that is going on around them – these dogs are a pleasure to take into the ring. In other cases, you need to encourage them along. In the UK and American show rings, this is often achieved by 'baiting' the dogs with small pieces of cooked liver. With this method, you take your Boxer in basic show pose and then tempt him with the liver in one hand while lifting his tail with the other. Have a look at the photo illustrating this style of handling on page 44 and it will become clear. The main thing to remember with this approach is that you are 'baiting' the dog with occasional small bits of food; you are not feeding him. When the judge comes around he or she wants to see the dog's head, not a mouthful of liver and drools of saliva. If you are not putting any other dog off, you may find that the action of dropping the bit of liver just in front of your Boxer at the precise moment when the judge is checking your dog's outline may well produce a very pleasing end result. But remember, please do pick up any piece of food that you drop in the ring.

Another method which some Boxers respond to very well is 'stringing'. In this

Ch. Vancroft's Primetime is being strung by his talented handler, Kay Palade.

case, you take your basic show pose and then place the choker under the dog's neck, holding it a couple of inches above his head. The photo above illustrates the end result of this technique clearly. If it is done

James Bettis is using small pieces of bait at the same time as he is stringing Ch. Cayman's Black Bart. The result is very effective.

properly on the right dog, he will lean forward into the choker and arch his neck beautifully, but he will be putting very little pressure on the chain itself since he will be standing in a very balanced manner. In carrying off this technique, you must make certain that you do not allow the chain to bunch up the skin beneath the chin. This is most unsightly and any loose skin should be pulled down behind the chain.

I think that stringing produces a very dramatic effect and, for the top American handlers, it is an art form which they have perfected. Many of them use very small bits of bait to accentuate the arch of neck and the dog's response still further. However, if it is done badly, the end result can be truly horrendous, with the dog straining against the chain, his neck backing down into his shoulders. If you are going to attempt to string a dog, he must be balanced and he must be made to get used to the feel of the chain around his neck from a very early age.

You cannot expect to get a dog to six months and then decide that you would like to have go at stringing him.

In other parts of the world, Boxers are shown on loose leads either by sparring up to each other or just by displaying inherent showmanship and poise. The photos showing dogs free-standing are wonderful, I think you will agree? The free showing Boxer is highly appreciated by judges and spectators alike, so, if your dog is such a natural that you can encourage him to perform in this way in the ring, you are a very lucky handler indeed. However, it often seems that the people who do try loose-lead showing in this country are doing so, not because they or their dog have any particular talent for it, but more because they cannot make any of the other techniques work. In these instances, the end result is not likely to be very good. It takes a real rapport between dog and handler to make it work and to ensure that the dog looks animated and balanced. Again, some of the professionals lead the way – I have never seen anyone do it better than the famous handler Christine Baum with the outstanding US Boxer bitch of the 90s, Ch. Kiebla's Tradition of TuRo.

The type of handling you select will be down to your own preference, but qualified by the dog's own capabilities. As I discuss in the chapter on showing, the best way of consolidating your technique is to attend the match nights which breed clubs put on. In addition, watch experienced handlers at work in the ring – making the best of their dog's virtues and trying to minimise any faults they might have. You can also help yourself by carrying out your training sessions at home in front of a full-length mirror so that you can clearly see the end

FREE STANDING

RIGHT: *Abgar von Bernamariek of Marbelton.*

BELOW: *Ch. Lounsbury's Flashback to Rupik.*

BELOW RIGHT: *Ch. Carinya Rye 'n' Dry.*

result of your efforts. Dogs can often feel wonderful when you are handling them, but this is not the most important consideration – they must look wonderful to the judge too!

You must also get your show Boxer to move accurately and with enthusiasm. When you have finished practising the stack, you should move him in a manner which replicates the show ring, i.e. an anti-clockwise triangle, with the dog maintaining a straight line and moving on your left-hand side. When you are moving your dog, get someone to watch him for you so that you can establish an optimum pace, and remember that your Boxer's

In the UK, your dog must get used to being benched during his days at Championship shows. Ch. Marbelton Dressed to Kill, a seasoned campaigner, takes it all in his stride.

optimum speed is likely to be faster in profile than it is coming and going. If you have difficulty getting your Boxer to move in a straight line, have a couple of training sessions with him moving in between you and a long, straight wall. This usually makes the message sink in. Please do not forget to train your dog to move correctly as well as to stand; a lot of people seem to put all their efforts into training their dogs to stand like statues, then seem to forget that they have to move as well!

Show training for dogs is best done young and regularly. By the time you get the dog into the ring at six months, the groundwork will have been done and regular attendance at shows will keep your Boxer in form without the real need for formal training to continue. However, do feel free to give him a refresher session now and again.

Finally, as part of his training, your puppy should be well-used to a crate, as these are very useful accessories at unbenched shows. At his first benched show, he must get used to sitting quietly and steadily on his bench. Some people feel the need to sit with their puppies all day, but I have to say that we find ours take to it very easily and, although we check regularly and never go far, we do let them get on with it. It will not always be practical to supervise dogs all day and once they have got used to your company it will be hard to break them of the habit.

4 ADULT MANAGEMENT

However much you like having a Boxer around, not everyone is going to share your enthusiasm and, in recent years, the level of controlling legislation and negative publicity surrounding dog ownership has increased exponentially. To play your part in combating this, it is vital that your dogs cause as little inconvenience or annoyance to other members of the public as possible. There is no doubt that this is best achieved by effective early training to make certain that you end up with a well-socialised companion. This will earn many friends for your dog and will reflect well on you as the owner.

In fact, I believe that showing consideration towards others takes very little effort in our easy-going breed and, principally, it involves always cleaning up after your dog when out walking, making sure that he knows how to greet house guests appropriately, never allowing his barking to become irritating, and ensuring that he is not allowed to worry other dogs or animals when being exercised free. This is only common sense and makes everyone's life a lot easier.

A beautiful, good-natured Boxer male.

Photo: Marcia.

Finally, I am a very firm believer that responsible ownership also means making sure that your dogs are covered by a suitable third-party liability insurance policy. None of us knows what is around the corner and you must make sure that you are fully covered in the unlikely event that your dog causes any serious accident or damage.

HOUSING

This is a 'people' breed and they need lots of human contact, so the home environment is undoubtedly the one in which Boxers thrive best, where they can be fully included in everyday family life. This does not necessarily mean that your Boxer has to be with you 100 per cent of the time and you will probably find it helpful to have somewhere that he can be left for a small part of the day. This may be your utility room or kitchen or a kennel and run in the garden, which is my own preference because I think that it does dogs good to spend at least some of their day out in the fresh air. As well as being convenient for you, it is important for your Boxer that he has some place in your home which he can call his own. Like humans, dogs need some personal space where they can occasionally get away from the hustle and bustle.

Although the home is the ideal environment for the Boxer, it often happens, especially if you are interested in showing, that numbers can quickly edge up when you start keeping the odd promising youngster for the ring. Very soon, it can become impracticable to keep all your dogs in the house, and kennels become a necessity. However, the breed's requirement for human companionship will always remain strong and, although it will be harder to fulfil in the kennel environment, you must put in the effort to make certain that you do have enough time and commitment to keep giving individual attention to all your dogs. For this reason, I do not think that Boxers are a breed which can be kept in very large numbers and I strongly believe that 10-12 Boxers is the maximum number that should be kept in a kennel. Also, I do not think that any dog should have to spend his entire life in kennels and, at the very least, every Boxer deserves the opportunity of spending his retirement years in a family home where he very soon learns to appreciate a few creature comforts. Do bear these two points in mind if you are intent on building up a kennel of your own.

As for the kennels and runs themselves, these should be located as near to the house as practicable for the benefit of the dogs and for your own convenience. This is especially true for your puppy run. It is also sensible to make sure that your chosen location does have some shade in the summer months. The base of the runs should definitely be constructed of concrete, gently sloping towards a drainage channel to ensure easy hosing down. Concrete is sturdy, easy to keep clean and good for the dogs' feet and nails. Standing on this base, the best runs are made of rigid weld-mesh frames and gates which bolt together in a firm structure and stand a few centimetres off the concrete, allowing water and debris to drain off freely. There is a large number of specialist manufacturers of suitable mesh who advertise regularly in the canine press. You will often find that delivery and erection is part of the service. Boxers, even if they are not the best of friends, do not usually bother each other

Boxers need lots of individual attention, so they cannot be kept successfully in very large numbers.

through the wire but, if you are concerned, you can purchase solid or semi-solid panels for the dividers between runs. Personally, I think it is much more pleasant for the dogs to be able to see each other and everything that is going on rather than looking at blank walls.

With such an active breed I do like to see big runs, though this does of course depend on how much other exercise you will be giving the dogs during the course of a day. It is sometimes useful to have at least one smaller run to accommodate the overactive adolescent who would be in danger of running himself out of condition in a large pen. By way of example, none of the main runs for our adult dogs is less than 23 feet long by 16 feet wide and, although I am prepared to believe that this is a bit over the top, I would not keep a Boxer in a run less than 13 feet by 7 feet. Although Boxers can be excellent jumpers, we usually find that if

they have been brought up in kennels they very rarely try to jump out, and runs 6 feet high are more than adequate.

Each run must also have a kennel where the dogs sleep and can shelter from the elements. There is a bit of a compromise here since a kennel is often easier to keep clean if you can stand up in it, but a smaller one is cosier for the dog. We go for wooden kennels which stand a couple of inches off the ground and are about five feet long long, broad and tall with the small access 'pop hole' sheltered from the prevailing wind. This enables us to shut our dogs in during the night and, with kennels this size, reasonably high-sided beds and proper bedding, we find that healthy, well-fed adult dogs conserve their body heat very effectively and do not require supplementary heating, even in the UK winter. Of course, puppies are a different matter altogether and you must also be prepared to heat your kennels if the dogs live partly in the house, as they will not be completely acclimatised to life out of doors. When necessary, we find that a dull-emitter lamp suspended a few feet over the kennel beds proves the most effective form of heating, directing the benefit exactly where it is needed.

As part of your kennel set-up you should also incorporate an isolation kennel, away from the main block, where you can house any dog with an infectious condition in an attempt to prevent it spreading. Of course, dogs who are under the weather will require heated accommodation and, if a dog needs nursing, please do think about bringing the invalid straight into the house until he is better. We have found that this always has a dramatic effect on a dog's speed of recovery, especially because their need for human company and reassurance is at its maximum when they are unwell.

I also view a dog kitchen-cum-utility room as an absolute must for your kennel. This is where we prepare all the dinners, keep the separate freezer for our dogs' meat, plastic sealed bins for their meal, a washing machine for their bedding and a shower area to bath them in. This type of general-purpose room is a godsend. You will also need to have somewhere secluded and quiet where your bitches can whelp. Again, if this can be a separate room attached to the house, then so much the better since you will then find it much easier to keep a close eye on your bitch and puppies and it will be more easily heated.

Outside, if space allows away from the main kennel block, a securely fenced and grassed exercise paddock will save you many hours. The capacity of a group of Boxers to amuse themselves endlessly in a facility like this never ceases to amaze me and, although it is not a complete substitute for proper walking, it can considerably reduce the amount you have to do – quite a benefit if you have a number of dogs.

Finally, to add the finishing touches to your kennel, you ought to make sure that it benefits from excellent external lighting, which will make your return from winter dog shows so much easier. It is sad, but, in this day and age, you must secure your property and kennels carefully, doing all that you can to prevent the possible theft of any of your dogs or puppies. Make no mistake, this crime is much more common than you might have thought. We have experienced it twice in the last five years and no experience is more soul-destroying.

As you can see, building a kennel set-up is no straightforward exercise and not many people have the time or money to do everything in one go, so plan carefully, start on a small scale, build things up gradually and, above all, check out the relevant planning and environmental health regulations with your local authority. Before you start to do anything, you must be fully acquainted with the ever-changing laws and inspection requirements covering the multiple ownership of dogs.

FEEDING

The first essential part of your routine must be to ensure that your Boxer has access to plenty of clean, fresh drinking water at all times. In a kennel environment, this usually means attaching the water bowl securely to the mesh, as one of the Boxers' favourite pastimes is to try and up-end their bowls as soon as you have filled them and then chase them all round the kennel!

Although we do continue to watch

Careful feeding pays dividends. Ch Socotra's Royal Game is an example of a beautifully conditioned Boxer. Photo: Pearce.

quantities and supplements carefully, our puppies have basically graduated to an adult diet by the time they are six months old, since we continue to feed all our dogs twice a day. This is partly to provide double excitement in the kennels and partly to ensure that we do not run the risk of overloading the dogs' digestion. Gastric torsion or bloat is a most dangerous ailment and prevention is far better than battling to cure it.

Boxers are good trenchermen, and getting your dog to eat voraciously should not be difficult. For our adults, we use a very straightforward method of feeding. In the morning we give each dog a pound of fresh minced tripe, followed in the late afternoon by another pound of tripe mixed with a slightly greater volume of biscuit meal which has been pre-soaked with boiling water. Then to conclude the day, we tend to give each dog a couple of biscuits when we shut them in for the night, though I have to admit that this is more of a bribe to ensure they rush into the kennel rather than a dietary requirement, but at least they go to bed happy. Fresh meat is easily obtained from pet stores, simply needing to be defrosted in a bucket of water prior to feeding and there is an ever-expanding range of dog biscuit to choose from.

Necessarily, the quantities I have given here are averages since different dogs, like humans, have slightly different requirements and you must obviously look at your stock carefully on a day-to-day basis, tailoring the precise amount of food given to the individual dog. On this score, you are fortunate that it is very easy to manage the weight on a Boxer, and you will be able to increase or decrease condition within a few days at the most. There is no real excuse for having either a thin dog or a fat one

We find that our feeding regime suits us well. It is very economical and the dogs thrive on it, with glossy coats, damp noses and clear eyes. But whenever I chat with other breeders I am always struck by the fact that we all feed our dogs in different ways and yet most show dogs are in comparable condition, thus proving that Boxers will do well on a whole variety of foods. In particular, a significant development in recent years has been the explosion in the use of complete foods, which many pet owners and kennels are now using very successfully and which must be the easiest way of feeding a dog and ensuring that he is getting a totally balanced diet.

Against a background of such wide-ranging choice in the current pet food market, the simple message on feeding must be to take the advice of your pup's breeder in the first instance (who is bound to have more practical experience of feeding Boxers than any commissioned salesman, vet or pet store owner) and, as long as your pup continues to look well, stick with his or her recommendations. It is always best to continue with a successful formula once you have found it, because dogs are not human-like in their approach to food and they do not appreciate unnecessary changes in their diet.

EXERCISE

An adult Boxer loves a good walk with plenty of free running exercise and, if you can take two together, then they will play endlessly, running each other off their feet. However, although your Boxer will always seem ready for more, moderation in all things must still be the motto. I think that you should aim to give your adults about half an hour of free running exercise daily. When doing this, do not be tempted to take them out in the heat of the day since you will all enjoy your walk so much more in the cool of the evening or first thing in the morning. You must also be careful never to exercise your dog immediately after he has eaten; let his dinner settle first and take him out a couple of hours later.

If you are showing your dog, there are one or two further considerations. It is certainly best to try and avoid any type of exercise which builds up some muscles disproportionately to others, or which places undue strain on certain parts of the anatomy; constant running up and down steep hills (or stairs) is the obvious example. You must also understand that exercising a show dog needs more attention at certain stages of canine development. For example, you may find that when faced with a gangly 'teenager' you have to put in a significant amount of daily roadwork to build up his musculation and co-ordination gradually, while limiting his free-running exercise to make sure that he does not run off all his condition. In fact, we always make any walk a combination of roadwork and free running. This discipline keeps the dog well-used to proper lead control and stops walks from developing into a mad rush, with the dog simply dragging you to the nearest field.

SLEEPING

Like all dogs, this is something that Boxers do a lot and so a good bed is essential. Dogs like to be secure when they are resting, and I think it is for this reason that they like the reassurance of feeling something around them – so do not be tempted to buy anything too large but go for the bed that they fit snugly into. Boxers

Kay Palade accompanies Ch. Vancroft's Primetime on a jog along the Florida beaches.

Boxers thrive on their creature comforts.

also seem to like resting their head and I have had most success with beds that have some sort of rim to them. Finally, I like dog beds to be raised a little way off the floor as this avoids the worst draughts. The base should be soft but firm to avoid any possible pressure sores, especially in the older dog. There are any number of products on the market that fulfil these criteria, from canine beanbags, which seem to be a great hit, to simpler moulded foam pads. However, if you are soft enough, you will find that the product which suits your Boxer's sleeping habits to perfection is an old armchair – if you can spare him one!

Actual choice of bed is not the only decision, since you now have to decide where to put it. You should find somewhere that your dog can retreat to, away from the noise of everyday household life and away from outside doors. Once you have decided on your location, leave the bed there, as this will be your dog's own personal space.

COMPANY
Boxers are a sociable breed and usually enjoy the company of others. In a kennel set-up, we always house our dogs in pairs

and they do become quite attached to one another. For this reason, we tend to stick with successful combinations and do not find that this gives us any problems when we are forced to arrange things differently, for example when bitches come into season. Just because a dog becomes used to living with one partner does not mean that he automatically goes off the rest of the kennel.

You hear all sorts of scare stories about keeping two males together (or two bitches), and the 'party line' always seems to be that the only sensible pairing is a dog and a bitch. I have to say, however, that we usually find little difficulty with any combination as long as you understand the dogs, are sensible about it and recognise that some Boxers are inherently more choosy than others. The only rule we do have is that we never house more than two adults together. Although you can usually exercise a few more together, three in a run is often problematic.

As far as the home environment goes, I like to have two Boxers together, and I think that they are almost easier to look after than one on its own, especially if they have to be left for a small part of the day.

Boxers usually enjoy each other's company. These three Winuwuk Champions are pictured while out on a country walk.

However, if you are going into Boxer ownership for the first time, this does not mean that you should be tempted to buy two puppies together since youngsters are a handful, even for an experienced owner. Start with one, and when your pup has reached adulthood and you have enjoyed the experience of bringing him up, you can then consider adding another, which you will find a lot easier – partly because you will have learnt from your mistakes first time around, and partly because your new puppy will quickly learn the ropes from your adult.

If keeping more than one dog, you must also recognise and avoid possible flashpoints. Introducing future partners is the first one – you should allow dogs to meet for the first time away from the 'territory' of either. If they are both old enough, the easiest way to introduce a pair is often to take them for a walk together. The second potential flashpoint is feeding, where bowls should be placed as far apart as possible. You should supervise your dogs when they are eating to make sure that one does not start stealing the other's food, though it is not unusual (when both have largely finished) for them to swap bowls just to check that there are no tidbits left. You must also be careful to show equal attention to both, as favouritism breeds contempt. I once committed all the sins simultaneously by bringing a new companion straight into the home with no warning for the existing resident; I then proceeded to allow the newcomer to sleep on the settee, a pleasure always denied to my other dog. I also fed them in a particularly cavalier fashion. Over a few weeks, resentment built up and a 'falling out' quickly followed. I will certainly not make the same mistakes again and I hope that you, the reader, will never make them.

FIGHTS

If you follow the simple rules on keeping more than one Boxer and if you carefully avoid the possible flashpoints, any fights will be very few and far between. Prevention is undoubtedly the best solution. However, from time to time, things will go wrong and you will have a fight on your hands. It is most important that you keep calm – getting hysterical will do nothing to help matters. Thankfully, Boxer fights are usually more noise than anything else and invariably sound far worse than they actually are. Do not be tempted to drag the dogs away from each other if they are locked on, as this risks tear wounds. The name of the game is to get the dogs to release their hold first. I usually find that a sharp hand grip applied very firmly and very swiftly to the scruff of the neck, accompanied simultaneously by a suitably loud and piercing "What do you think you're doing?" is enough, momentarily, to make the dog let go, allowing you to pull him off safely. If there is someone else there to do the same to the other party, so much the better, as some assistance makes sure that when you get the dogs apart, they stay apart. In more determined fights, you may need to be a little more inventive – water from a hosepipe directed at the dog's face normally makes him let go, and so does a quantity of pepper released around the dog's nose. The one thing you must watch is that you have a firm hold when the dog does let go, since it is not unheard of that in the frenzy of the moment the Boxer releases his grip on his opponent and simply grabs the next available object – you need to make sure that this is not you.

After a fight is over and the dogs have returned to their senses, you will usually find that they are a bit ashamed of themselves and have that innocent, sheepish look. It is also uncommon for two Boxers to maintain a long-term grudge after a punch-up, and you will often find that the two parties are reconcilable. However, you should certainly not assume this and you will need to use your common sense in never allowing fights between pairs to become a regular occurrence. In my view, twice is regular. Do also remember to check your dogs over after the event and to disinfect any puncture wounds. Boxers heal up quickly and serious injury requiring veterinary advice after a fight is unusual.

BARKING

Thankfully, well-socialised Boxers are a very sensible breed when it comes to barking and, even with a few together, they rarely become a noise nuisance. Given this breed characteristic, it is always sensible to investigate matters immediately when your Boxer does bark, as it will invariably be for a reason. If you are unlucky and have ended up with a noisy one (which has been known), there are excellent collars on sale which emit a strong scent when the dog barks. These can prove very effective in shutting them up.

GROOMING AND BATHING

With his short, fine coat, the Boxer finds it easy to keep himself clean and tidy and he will need very little help from you. A quick once-over with the grooming glove each week is quite enough and, as long as your dog is in good condition and you have his diet right, you will notice that his coat positively gleams and he sheds very little.

As far as baths are concerned, I have to say that I do not subscribe to the widely-held belief that adult Boxers do not need bathing more than once or twice a year. With the best will in the world, and especially in wetter climates, dogs can develop quite an unusual aroma. As far as house dogs are concerned, I tend to bath them at least once a month in a mixture of half insecticidal canine shampoo and half normal shampoo/conditioner. The dogs love the attention, jump in the bath of their own free will and seem to enjoy being freshened up. I suppose it is all a matter of personal preference, but baths will certainly do nothing to harm the dog – you just need to make sure that you apply the common sense rules of keeping the shampoo and the water away from their eyes and ears and making sure that they are kept warm and draught-free until they are fully dry.

ROUTINE HEALTH CARE

We will be looking at health care more thoroughly later, but there are a few regular tasks that you need to carry out to make sure that your Boxer remains in peak condition. I always think that it is sensible to use your dog's weekly grooming session as a good opportunity to do a quick health check, when you should be keeping a close lookout for anything out of the ordinary.

On this weekly basis, you should check the coat for any unwelcome visitors and have a look in the ears. You may find, especially if you have a cat, that your Boxer faces a constant battle with ear mites, so this is a most important check, as ears are easily kept clean if monitored and treated regularly. Any eye abnormality is also much better treated at a very early stage, so do have a look there as well. Eyes should be clear and bright, with any cloudiness brought to the attention of your vet.

You should have a look at the dog's teeth to see that they are clean and that his breath remains fresh. You should also look down at your Boxer's feet to ensure that the nails are short and trim. If he is a young dog being exercised properly, then you should have to do very little on this score, but do keep an eye on the older dog. Few things are more uncomfortable than long nails and, once you have let them go, they are difficult to get back in order. Some people find they get on better with the neat electric nail grinders you can buy these days, rather than the more traditional cutters, and there seems to be less chance of digging too deep and hurting the dog.

NEUTERING

There can be no doubt that the number of unwanted dogs and litters these days provides a strong case for the neutering of family pets, but I am a little perturbed by the limited amount of thought that owners sometimes give to this. It is a fact that castrating a dog or, in particular, spaying a bitch is a major surgical procedure under general anaesthetic and therefore not one that should be undertaken lightly – especially as far as Boxers are concerned. In common with all of the shorter-nosed breeds, anaesthetics need to be administered with some care.

When faced with totally responsible owners, who keep their dogs under proper control, I do not understand why neutering is often recommended so routinely. It is debatable whether it changes temperament fundamentally (often quoted as the reason for castrating a male), and it does seem much more difficult to control a Boxer's weight after the operation has been done. It may make life easier not having to cope with a bitch's seasons twice a year, but, in this instance, are you doing it for the bitch's benefit or for your own?

All I would ask when you are making your decision on this important subject is to think about it logically, and do not let yourself be bullied into a politically correct decision. There are valid reasons for and against, but the arguments in favour always seem to be given more prominence these days.

THE ADOLESCENT

Puppyhood is undoubtedly a vital period of character building but, as far as training goes, I believe that adolescence is an even more important time in a Boxer's life. The breed is essentially dominant in character and, in simple language, this means that they like to be in control – so, if you, as the owner, are not in charge, they will quickly take over. The period between 12 and 18 months is when your Boxer is most likely to get a little headstrong, the males in particular, and you need to take a firm line. This does not mean physical chastisement; it simply means sticking to your guns and making sure that the dog knows who is boss.

This Boxer bitch is ten years old and still full of fun.

THE VETERAN

Boxers actually have a comparatively short period of old age, remaining youthful for such a long time, with their boundless energy and zest for life. However, their pensionable years do come around in time, marked by a few distinguished grey hairs on the muzzle, a slight slowing-down caused by physical stiffness rather than a lack of willingness, and a little (partly selective?) deafness.

When these signs become apparent, you just need to be a little more sensitive to your dog's needs. Your exercising regime should be tailored to fit in with the old dog's needs – he still needs to be kept active and fit, but he should not go perhaps quite as far as he used to. He will still enjoy the company of other dogs, but you should make sure that any younger dogs you have are not allowed to pester him constantly or challenge his position as top dog. It is also sensible to feed him in smaller quantities, as well as more regularly, so that his slower digestion is not placed on overload. Naturally, you need to keep an even closer eye on general health and condition than you did when he was younger.

I must say that there is no better household pet than an older Boxer, and you should treasure these final years with a companion who knows your every move, and who seems wiser than you ever thought a dog could be. However, the one thing you must never do is prolong your Boxer's old age for your benefit alone. Pride and dignity are the two most important things to an old Boxer, and he must never be denied them. Euthanasia at the right time is possibly the kindest thing an owner can do, and I can assure you that in your heart of hearts you will know when the time is right. Never allow yourself to put it off, in the hope that nature will take its course and save you the decision.

5 *HEALTH CARE*

The chances are that you are not medically qualified in any shape or form – I know I am not – and, because of this, you will be heavily reliant on your vet to keep your Boxer in good health. However, your vet cannot do this alone and you need to share responsibility with him. Your job is to use common sense, and recognise anything slightly out of the ordinary and any possible symptoms of illness at an early stage. It is always better to seek veterinary advice sooner rather than later and the best advice I can give you is to go with your first instincts.

On a number of occasions, we have looked at our Boxers and thought "I don't know, you don't seem quite right to me," but then put it out of our mind because they have quickly jumped up to say hello and have apparently resumed normal activities. However, 99 times out of 100 if you find yourself thinking this way, you will have noticed something odd, no matter how imperceptible, and it is best to get things checked out. I know we once fell into the trap of not doing so and we almost lost a bitch with pyometra. Boxers are the most stoical of breeds and they withstand

great pain in silence. It is for this reason that you must always be on the lookout for indicators that all is not well: a slight loss of vigour; changes in normal routine; changes in eating and drinking patterns; any sign of lameness; a look of discomfort; running eyes and a dry nose; or the more obvious signs of vomiting, diarrhoea, weight loss and excessive tiredness.

A useful aid to you will be a canine thermometer to check the dog's temperature, and it is often helpful to know this before you phone the vet. You should always disinfect the thermometer before use and, while the dog is standing, it should be inserted into his rectum and held there for about a minute. The normal temperature for a dog is 38.5 degrees C or 101.5 degrees F.

CHOOSING A VET
I have the greatest respect for veterinary practitioners and, over the years, we have had a succession of excellent vets who have been outstanding professionally and who have also been willing to listen to our own opinions, as breeders who have more experience of living with Boxers on a day-

*This fine Boxer,
Ch. Bandelero, is
clearly in peak
physical condition.*

to-day basis. A relationship between breeder and vet, in which both parties are prepared to listen and learn from each other, has lots to recommend it.

It is also important that you have a vet who actually understands the breed. Very occasionally, you hear absolute horror stories about vets wanting to operate on Boxers to 'correct' their naturally undershot jaws, or pressurising clients unacceptably on the issues of docking, line-breeding or Caesareans. Needless to say, these vets are very few and far between and they are best avoided. I think that excessive political correctness in a vet is a very undesirable characteristic.

If you live in the same locality as your Boxer's breeder, then it may be sensible to use the same veterinary practice or, if you have to make the decision yourself, remember that you can always move your custom elsewhere if you do not quite see eye to eye with your first choice. The only other piece of advice I would give is to check now and again that the fees being charged by your chosen practice are comparable to the local competition. There

can be a significant variation and there is no real excuse for this, especially when it comes to routine tasks such as neutering and vaccinations. I always believe that none of us should ever resent any money spent at the vet, because peace of mind has no price but, deep down, I think we all like to know that we are not being taken for a ride financially.

COMMON AILMENTS
This is not meant to be an exhaustive list, and some health issues connected with

*Donnymoor
Simply the
Best. Boxers
are naturally
undershot –
don't let your
vet tell you
any different!*

whelping are covered in Chapter Ten. I have also deliberately left distemper, viral hepatitis, leptospirosis and parvovirus off the list, since your Boxer should never experience these serious conditions if you have him correctly vaccinated and regularly boosted.

ANAL GLANDS: In a healthy dog, these glands empty naturally when the dog defecates but, if they become impacted, they will need to be emptied by hand. An impacted anal gland can cause the dog considerable discomfort and he will often drag his bottom along the ground as a result. Emptying these glands is not a pleasant task, but it is one that you will be able to carry out yourself when you have watched the vet do it once and have armed yourself beforehand with plastic gloves and some cotton wool. By way of prevention, a higher-fibre diet can help.

BLOAT: This is when the digestive system overloads and the stomach becomes distended with gas. The affected dog will normally be very restless and make unproductive attempts to vomit. The enlarged stomach will very soon press on the diaphragm, resulting in a dramatic shortness of breath and, from the outside, the belly can feel like a balloon. This is a very serious condition as it can very quickly cause the stomach to twist, resulting in gastric torsion. It is an emergency and requires immediate veterinary attention.

CHEYLETIELLA: Also known as 'walking dandruff', this mite is usually seen as excessive scurf. It is highly contagious and readily transferable to humans, though, thankfully, it is not very pathogenic on

either man or beast. Your vet will be able to prescribe a suitable preparation which will need to be applied at regular intervals on all the animals in the household to clear the environment.

COLITIS: This is inflammation of the colon, usually indicated by a dog straining to pass faeces which appear to have a jelly coating and which also have fresh blood in them. Several causes can lie behind this and the condition will need to be investigated by your vet. Some cases can be corrected simply by a change of diet, but in other instances the causes are more serious.

CONSTIPATION: If your dog is experiencing difficulty in passing faeces, a dessertspoonful of medicinal liquid paraffin usually does the trick. Constipation can sometimes be caused by a lack of fluid intake or too much dry food in the diet. Consult your vet if it persists.

COPROPHAGIA: The unpleasant habit of dogs eating their own faeces can come as quite a shock when owners experience it for the first time but, thankfully, it is comparatively rare in Boxers. Prevention is the best cure – by getting there to clean up before the dog has a chance to tuck in. Another method worth a try is adding fresh pineapple to the dog's diet.

DIARRHOEA: If the dog's temperature is normal, then this is likely to have been caused by something that the dog has eaten, and twelve hours without food (but with continued access to water) should sort things out, together with a children's dose of kaolin and morphine. However, if it is accompanied by a temperature, if it persists for more than 24 hours, or if there are signs of blood in the faeces, please do consult your vet. As you become more experienced, you will quickly be able to distinguish between a passing attack and something more serious.

EAR MITES: These affect the inside of the ear and cause the dog to shake his head and scratch his ears. On further investigation, you will find that the inside of the ear is grubby and brown. Boxers seem particularly prone to these, especially if they live with cats, and you must keep a constant check. Your vet will be able to give you the appropriate ear drops to treat the dog as well as any cats you might have.

EPILEPSY: A disease caused by abnormal electrical activity in the brain, leading to recurrent fits. If your dog has a fit, do not interfere while the fit is progressing but do your best to try and stop him from injuring himself by moving nearby objects. You should also try and remember the sequence of events precisely so that you can subsequently describe them to your vet. This is a most distressing condition for owners but, up to a point, it can be managed by prescribed medication.

EYE ULCERS: The initial signs are a partially-closed eyelid and excess tear production, and the start of the ulcer can usually be seen as a grey dot on the eye. Do act early when you spot these signs and get your vet to look at it immediately, because the sooner they are caught, the less difficult they are to treat. In extreme cases the dog may need his eye sewn up for a while, but quick action can usually avoid this.

Wardo v Dommeldal of Tyegarth. Clear, sparkling eyes are a sure sign that all is well.
Photo: Smethurst.

FLEAS: Black dots of flea dirt in the dog's coat are usually easier to detect than the actual fleas and you will often be alerted to the presence of fleas when your dog starts scratching persistently. Treat the dog with a flea spray from your vet and do the same to his bedding as well.

GROWTHS: Boxers are notoriously prone to little lumps and bumps, especially in old age, so, although you should not worry unnecessarily, get your vet to have a look. Some are best left well alone, while others will need to come off.

KENNEL COUGH: The most important thing to recognise is that you do not need a kennel to get kennel cough; it merely acquired this name because it spreads so contagiously among a group of dogs. I always think of it as like the common cold in humans, because it is characterised by a running nose and an unmistakable hacking cough. Several different viruses are involved and a specific bacterium is often found in the trachea. Your vet will be able to give some remedies to moderate the symptoms and, for your part, you should limit the dog's exercise and excitement. It is not usually a serious illness in physically strong adults, but it can be dangerous in the young and the old. It tends to last a couple of weeks and, during this time, you must try not to let your dog come into contact with others. Thankfully, once a dog has suffered Kennel Cough, he does not tend to get it again and there are now some excellent vaccines available. These do not give 100 per cent protection, but they do seem to shorten the length and severity of the illness.

LAMENESS: Watch your dog very carefully when he is moving to identify where the problem lies – this is sometimes easier said than done – and then examine the affected leg carefully, checking for any abnormality, which might be nail problems, a cut pad, cysts between the toes or any unusual swelling or puffiness. Lameness in a Boxer is usually about as short-lived as it is on the football pitch when a striker is playing for a penalty.

LYME DISEASE: This is probably transmitted by certain ticks and results in fever, bad appetite and recurrent arthritis in certain joints. Your vet will be able to prescribe a suitable antibiotic. This condition is, thankfully, comparatively rare in the UK, but more common in America.

MANGE: There are various types, but mange is basically an infestation of parasitic mites which causes skin disease, sometimes causing partial hair loss and often accompanied by secondary infection after the dog has continually scratched itself with discomfort. Your vet will be able to recommend a suitable wash.

PYOMETRA: This is where the uterus fills with pus and this pus may either be retained inside by a closed cervix (closed pyometra), or it may appear at the vulva (open pyometra). Most commonly, it occurs in bitches up to ten weeks after their season. Closed pyometra is harder to detect, but increased thirst and a bad appetite are classic signs. It can also be accompanied by the bitch looking 'tucked up' and stiff. This is a very serious condition which needs quick veterinary attention and, although it can be cured without surgery, the majority of cases require a hysterectomy.

SKELETAL SCURVY: We went through a phase in Boxers a few years ago when this unpleasant condition kept popping up, and we have certainly had the occasional case in our own kennel. It normally occurs in puppies between three and seven months of age, and it is characterised by hot swellings around the joints, especially the pastern joints of the front legs. The pain will often be so bad that the puppy will scream if you touch the affected area and he will be very reluctant to stand up. You will also find that his temperature has rocketed to 104-105F. It is true to say that a lot of uncertainty surrounds this condition, though it was thought at one point that it resulted from a lack of Vitamin C. More likely is the theory that there is some abnormality in the dog's production of Vitamin C, prompted by the overfeeding of other vitamins and minerals. Veterinary attention is immediately required.

STINGS: If your dog is stung by a bee, you will need to extract the sting with tweezers, if it is still lodged, before bathing with a bicarbonate of soda solution. If it is a wasp sting, bathe with water and vinegar. If the sting is located in or near the dog's mouth, seek veterinary attention and apply a pack of frozen peas to the affected area to prevent swelling in the meantime.

SUNSTROKE: Although they are comparatively short-nosed, Boxers do not fare too badly in the sun, but, if they do ever overheat, it is important to lower the body temperature immediately. Apply ice packs or packs of frozen peas to the back of the neck and the skull area and, if necessary, hose the dog down. If your dog is overheating, his natural panting will become very laboured and the noise created will change into a type of 'roaring' sound. Prevention is undoubtedly the best line of attack, so do not walk your dog when it is too hot and avoid car journeys in the heat of the day.

TEETH: Signs of dental disease include foul breath and excessive salivation. If these symptoms occur, check the mouth for signs of reddening at the junction between the teeth and the gums and look for any brown spots on the teeth themselves. Consult your vet if you suspect problems.

TICKS: The most common in the UK are sheep ticks, which appear as a grey dot when they first attach themselves and dig their heads into the flesh. They become much more visible once they have engorged with blood. You should not simply pull them away from the dog as this will still leave their head embedded and could lead to an abscess. The tick should first be covered in white spirit or Vaseline, left for a while and then slowly extracted by lifting it from the neck.

WORMS: If your Boxer is eating well but not thriving, with poor coat condition and diarrhoea, he may be infested with worms. There are several different types of worm but the most common are roundworm and tapeworm. Although you can buy worm control products at pet shops, I believe that the prescription vermifuge obtainable from your vet is far more effective. As a preventative measure, adult dogs should be wormed twice a year and puppies, until they are three months old, should be wormed every two or three weeks.

FIRST AID KIT
It is always sensible to have a few basic supplies ready to cope with minor ailments. In our kennel we keep the following on hand: a canine thermometer (the ones with a digital display are a godsend); insecticidal shampoo; bandages and surgical tape; scissors; tweezers; disinfectant; skincare ointment (we tend to use Benzyl Benzoate); antiseptic cream; eyedrops; glucose powder; a supply of comfortable synthetic bedding; electrical heat pads; liquid paraffin and flea spray.

6 *THE BREED STANDARD*

After the very first Boxer show in 1896, the Munich Boxer Club set about the task of drawing up a Breed Standard. The ground for this exercise had already been prepared by Friedrich Roberth but, in spite of this, it took the Boxer Club six years to come up with a suitable wording. The first Standard was eventually adopted on January 14th 1902, but it was not to everyone's taste and various splinter groups went their own separate ways. However by 1905, all German clubs had agreed that the Standard drawn up by the Munich Boxer Club should be universally accepted and, to this day, all Boxer Standards track back to this original blueprint.

When the Boxer began to achieve popularity in English-speaking countries, the German document obviously needed translation; this was not easy and the process was also complicated by the fact that the German Standard went through several revisions in its early days. However, in 1936, Lilian Palmedo and her mother Ida Gaertner, who were both fluent German speakers and members of the American Boxer Club, helped the American Kennel Club to translate the Boxer Standard. The trouble was that the document on which they based their translation was either a very early German Standard (certainly pre-dating its major 1920 revision) or it was a copy of the Austrian Standard which existed before Austria came into line with Germany. The end result of their efforts was promptly adopted by the AKC before the wider membership of the Boxer Club had seen it. Of course, these members were all trying to import and breed dogs which conformed to the then current German Standard, not to the AKC's unorthodox translation, and so there was immediate dissension in the ranks. Jack Wagner was blunt in his own comments when he wrote in 1937: "The German Boxer is so new to America that most of our basic breeding stock is of German origin, with additional imports arriving almost daily. Under these conditions, the adoption by the AKC of its own standards, definitely differing from, rather than conforming to, the accepted German version was an unforgivable blunder bound to cause trouble."

However, the confusion was thankfully short-lived, because Philip Stockmann was scheduled to judge Boxers at Westminster in February 1938 and this provided a marvellous opportunity to resolve matters once and for all. A breed summit was convened between Herr Stockmann, Jack Wagner, Mesdames Palmedo and Gaertner, an AKC official and Enno Meyer. As a result of this meeting, a new translation of the current German Standard was adopted, with the exception of colour where the Americans continued to disqualify white and check Boxers. At the time, Germany was still allowing the registration of these colours, but they were soon to follow the American lead in order to ensure that their Boxers could attain working dog status. This new English translation of the German Standard was eventually sent over to Britain, where it was adopted without material change and, as far as the British Boxer Club was concerned, this swiftly settled its own difficulties in getting a Standard agreed. That 1938 meeting, attended by Philip Stockmann, had proved critical in achieving the early consensus which then allowed breeders to get on with the more pressing task of breeding typical Boxers.

Over the years, there have continued to be a number of revisions to the Boxer Standard in various countries and these have often been prompted by national Kennel Club directives. For example, the English Kennel Club recently decided that, for all breeds, it wanted less wordy Standards in a unified format. As far as the Boxer Standard is concerned, it has become fashionable to criticise the end result, which is significantly less descriptive than its predecessor, although the basic requirements have stayed the same. The Americans also unified their Standards in the late 1980s but, unlike the UK, the revised version was warmly received, being less repetitive and much clearer, but still remaining very true to its 1938 German roots. I reprint both Standards below. My own view is that the English Standard remains perfectly acceptable as a basic guide to the rights and wrongs, but I always think of it as a base document which needs some 'backing papers'. From an educational point of view, my strong preference is always for the American Standard, partly because of its history and partly because it was obviously written by people who understood and lived with the breed. At the end of the day, this description of a Boxer which was largely agreed upon by Philip Stockmann and Jack Wagner – two individuals of unquestioned authority – cannot be a bad place to start!

THE FULL UK STANDARD

General appearance: Great nobility, smooth-coated, medium-sized, square build, strong bone and evident, well developed muscles.

Characteristics: Lively, strong, loyal to owner and family, but distrustful of strangers. Obedient, friendly at play, but with guarding instinct.

Temperament: Equable, biddable, fearless, self-assured.

Head and skull: Head imparts its unique stamp and is in proportion to the body, appearing neither light nor too heavy. Skull lean without exaggerated cheek muscles. Muzzle broad, deep and

BASIC ANATOMY
Basic canine anatomy illustrated by
Ch. Roamaro Scotch Mist of Winuwuk,
a very well made Boxer bitch.

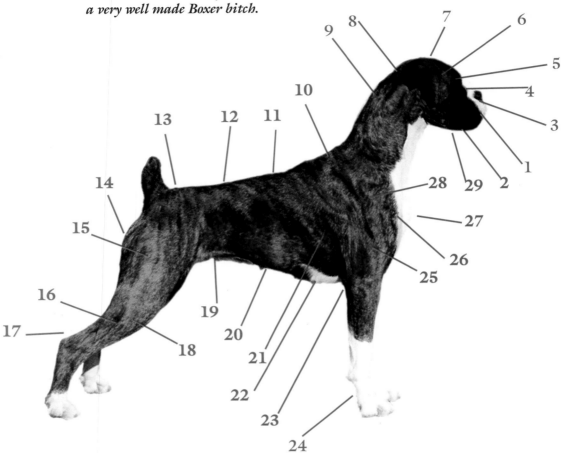

1. Chin	11. Back	21. Rib cage
2. Muzzle	12. Loin	22. Brisket
3. Nose	13. Croup	23. Elbow
4. Stop	14. Hip protuberance	24. Pastern
5. Forehead	15. Upper Thigh	25. Upper arm
6. Skull	16. Lower Thigh	26. Point of shoulder
7. Occiput	17. Hock	27. Forechest
8. Nape of neck	18. Stifle/knee	28. Shoulder blade
9. Neck	19. Tuck up	29. Flews
10. Withers	20. Underline	

powerful, never narrow, pointed, short or shallow. Balance of skull and muzzle essential, with muzzle never appearing small, viewed from any angle. Skull cleanly covered, showing no wrinkle, except when alerted. Creases present from root of nose running down sides of muzzle. Dark mask confined to muzzle, distinctly contrasting with colour of head, even when white is present. Lower jaw undershot, curving slightly upward. Upper jaw broad where attached to skull, tapering very slightly to front. Muzzle shape completed by upper lips, thick and well padded, supported by well separated canine teeth of lower jaw. Lower edge of upper lip rests on edge of lower lip, so that chin is clearly perceptible when viewed from front or side. Lower jaw never to obscure front of upper lip, neither should teeth nor tongue be visible when mouth closed. Top of skull slightly arched, not rounded, nor too flat and broad. Occiput not too pronounced. Distinct stop, bridge of nose never forced back into forehead, nor should it be downfaced. Length of muzzle measured from tip of nose to inside corner of eye is one-third the length of head measured from tip of nose to occiput. Nose broad, black, slightly turned up, wide nostrils with well defined line between. Tip of nose set slightly higher than root of muzzle. Cheeks powerfully developed, never bulging.

Eyes: Dark brown, forward looking, not too small, protruding or deeply set. Showing lively intelligent expression. Dark rims with good pigmentation showing no haw.

Ears: Moderate size, thin, set wide apart on highest part of skull, lying flat and close to cheek in repose, but falling forward with definite crease when alert.

Mouth: Undershot jaw, canines set wide apart with incisors (six) in straight line in lower jaw. In upper jaw set in line curving slightly forward. Bite powerful and sound, with teeth set in normal arrangement.

Neck: Round, of ample length, strong, muscular, clean cut, no dewlap. Distinctly marked nape and elegant arch down to withers.

Forequarters: Shoulders long and sloping, close lying, not excessively covered with muscle. Upper arm long, making right angle to shoulder blade. Forelegs seen from front, straight, parallel, with strong bone. Elbows not too close or standing too far from chest wall. Forearms perpendicular, long and firmly muscled. Pasterns short, clearly defined, but not distended, slightly slanted.

Body: In profile square, length from forechest to rear of upper thigh equal to height at withers. Chest deep, reaching to elbows. Depth of chest half height at withers. Ribs well arched, not barrel-shaped, extending well to rear. Withers clearly defined. Back short, straight, slightly sloping, broad and strongly muscled. Loin short, well tucked up and taut. Lower abdominal line blends into curve to rear.

Hindquarters: Very strong, with muscles

hard and standing out noticeably under skin. Thighs broad and curved. Broad croup, slightly sloped, with flat, broad arch. Pelvis long and broad. Upper and lower thigh long. Good hind angulation; when standing, the stifle is directly under the hip protuberance. Seen from the side, leg from hock joint to foot not quite vertical. Seen from behind, legs straight, hock joints clean, with powerful rear pads.

Feet: Front feet small and cat-like, with well arched toes, and hard pads; hind feet slightly longer.

Tail: Set on high, customarily docked and carried upward.

Gait/movement: Strong, powerful with noble bearing, reaching well forward, and with driving action of hindquarters. In profile, stride free and ground-covering.

Coat: Short, glossy, smooth and tight to body.

Colour: Fawn or brindle. White markings acceptable not exceeding one-third of ground colour. Fawn: Various shades from deer red to light fawn. Brindle: Black stripes on previously described fawn shades, running parallel to ribs all over body. Stripes contrast distinctly to ground colour, neither too close nor thinly dispersed. Ground colour clear, not intermingling with stripes.

Size: Height: dogs, 57-63 cms (22.5-25 ins); bitches, 53-59 cms (21-23 ins).

Weight: dogs, approximately 30-32 kgs (66-70 lbs); bitches, approximately 25-27 kgs (55-60 lbs).

Faults: Any departure from the foregoing points should be considered a fault and the seriousness with which the fault should be regarded should be in exact proportion to its degree.

Note: Male animals should have two apparently normal testicles fully descended into the scrotum.

Approved 1988

THE FULL US STANDARD

GENERAL APPEARANCE
The ideal Boxer is a medium-sized, square built dog of good substance with short back, strong limbs and short tight fitting coat. His well developed muscles are clean, hard and appear smooth under taut skin. His movements denote energy. The gait is firm, yet elastic, the stride free and ground-covering, the carriage proud. Developed to serve as guard, working and companion dog, he combines strength and agility with elegance and style. His expression is alert and temperament steadfast and tractable.

The chiselled head imparts to the Boxer a unique individual stamp. It must be in correct proportion to the body. The broad, blunt muzzle is the distinctive feature, and great value is placed upon its being of proper form and balance with the skull.

In judging the Boxer, first consideration is given to general appearance, to which attractive colour and arresting style may contribute. Next is overall balance with special attention devoted to the head, after which the individual body components are examined for their correct construction, and efficiency of gait evaluated.

SIZE, PROPORTION, SUBSTANCE

Height: Adult males 22.5 to 25 inches; females 21 to 23.5 inches at the withers. Preferably, males should not be under the minimum nor females over the maximum; however proper balance and quality in the individual should be of primary importance since there is no size disqualification.

Proportion: The body in profile is of square proportion in that a horizontal line from the front of the fore-chest to the rear projection of the upper thigh should equal the length of a vertical line dropped from the top of the withers to the ground.

Substance: Sturdy with balanced musculature. Males larger boned than their female counterparts.

HEAD
The beauty of the head depends upon harmonious proportion of muzzle to skull. The blunt muzzle is 1/3rd the length of the head from the occiput to the tip of the nose, and 2/3rds the width of the skull. The head should be clean, not showing deep wrinkles (wet). Wrinkles typically appear upon the forehead when ears are erect, and folds are always present from the lower edge

of the stop running downward on both sides of the muzzle.

Expression: Intelligent and alert.

Eyes: Dark brown in colour, not too small, too protruding or too deep-set. Their mood-mirroring character combined with the wrinkling of the forehead, gives the Boxer head its unique quality of expressiveness.

Ears: Set at the highest points of the sides of the skull are cropped, cut rather long and tapering, raised when alert.

Skull: The top of the skull is slightly arched, not rounded, flat nor noticeably broad, with the occiput not overly pronounced. The forehead shows a slight indentation between the eyes and forms a distinct stop with the topline of the muzzle. The cheeks should be relatively flat and not bulge (cheekiness), maintaining the clean lines of the skull, and should taper into the muzzle in a slight, graceful curve.

Muzzle: The muzzle, proportionately developed in length, width and depth, has a shape influenced first through the formation of both jaw-bones, second through the placement of the teeth, and third through the texture of the lips. The top of the muzzle should not slant down (downfaced), nor should it be concave (dishfaced); however, the tip of the nose should lie slightly higher than the root of the muzzle.

The nose should be broad and black.

The upper jaw is broad where attached to the skull and maintains this breadth except for a very slight tapering to the front. The lips, which complete the formation of the muzzle, should meet evenly in the front. The upper lip is thick and padded, filling out the frontal space created by the projection of the lower jaw. Therefore the canines must stand far apart and be of good length so that the front surface of the muzzle is broad and squareish and, when viewed from the side, shows moderate layback. The chin should be perceptible from the side as well as from the front.

Bite: The Boxer is undershot; the lower jaw protrudes beyond the upper and curves slightly upward. The incisor teeth of the lower jaw are in a straight line, with the canines preferably up front in the same line to give the jaw the greatest possible width. The upper line of incisors is slightly convex with the corner upper incisors fitting snugly back of the lower canine teeth on each side.

Faults: Skull too broad. Cheekiness. Wrinkling too deep (wet) or lacking (dry). Excessive flews. Muzzle too light for skull. Too pointed a bite (snipy), too undershot, teeth or tongue showing when mouth closed. Eyes noticeably lighter than ground colour of coat.

NECK, TOPLINE, BODY
Neck: Round, of ample length, muscular and clean without excessive hanging skin (dewlap). The neck has a distinctly marked nape with an elegant arch blending smoothly into the withers.

Topline: Smooth, firm and slightly sloping.

Body: The chest is of fair width, and the forechest well defined and visible from the side. The brisket is deep, reaching down to the elbows; the depth of the body at the lowest point of the brisket equals half the height of the dog at the withers. The ribs, extending far to the rear, are well arched but not barrel shaped.

The back is short, straight and muscular and firmly connects the withers to the hind quarters.

The loins are short and muscular.

The lower stomach is lightly tucked up, blending into a graceful curve to the rear. The croup is slightly sloped, flat and broad. Tail is set high, docked and carried upward. Pelvis long and in females especially broad.

Faults: Short, heavy neck. Chest too broad, too narrow or hanging between shoulders. Lack of forechest. Hanging stomach. Slab-sided rib cage. Long or narrow loin, weak union with croup. Falling off of croup. Higher in rear than in front.

FOREQUARTERS
The shoulders are long and sloping. Close-lying, and not excessively covered with muscle (loaded). The upper arm is long, approaching a right angle to the shoulder blade. The elbows should not press too closely to the chest wall nor stand off visibly from it.

The forelegs are long, straight and firmly muscled and, when viewed from the front, stand parallel to each other. The pastern is strong and distinct, slightly slanting, but standing almost perpendicular to the ground. The dewclaws may be removed. Feet should be compact, turning neither in nor out, with well arched toes.

Faults: Loose or loaded shoulders. Tied in or bowed out elbows.

HINDQUARTERS

The hindquarters are strongly muscled with angulation in balance with that of forequarters.

The thighs are broad and curved, the breech musculature hard and strongly developed. Upper and lower thigh long. Leg well angulated at the stifle with clearly defined, well 'let down' hock joint. Viewed from behind, the hind legs should be straight with hock joints leaning neither in nor out. From the side, the leg below the hock (metatarsus) should be almost perpendicular to the ground, with a slight slope to the rear permissible. The metatarsus should be short, clean and strong. The Boxer has no rear dewclaws.

Faults: Steep or over-angulated hindquarters. Light thighs or over-developed hams. Over-angulated (sickle) hocks. Hindquarters too far under or too far behind.

COAT

Short, shiny, lying smooth and tight to the body.

COLOUR

The colours are fawn and brindle. Fawn shades vary from light tan to mahogany. The brindle ranges from sparse, but clearly defined black stripes on a fawn background, to such a heavy concentration of black striping that the essential fawn background colour barely, although clearly, shows through (which may create the appearance of 'reverse brindling').

White markings should be of such distribution as to enhance the dog's appearance, but may not exceed one-third of the entire coat. They are not desirable on the flanks or on the back of the torso proper. On the face, white may replace part of the otherwise essential black mask and may extend in an upward path between the eyes, but it must not be excessive, so as to detract from true Boxer expression.

Faults: Unattractive or misplaced white markings.

Disqualifications: Boxers that are any colour other than fawn or brindle. Boxers with a total of white markings exceeding one-third of the entire coat.

GAIT

Viewed from the side, proper front and rear angulation is manifested in a smoothly efficient, level-backed, ground covering stride with powerful drive emanating from a freely operating rear. Although the front legs do not contribute impelling power, adequate 'reach' should be evident to prevent interference, overlap or 'sidewinding' (crabbing). Viewed from the front, the shoulders should remain trim and the elbows not flare out. The legs are parallel until the gait narrows the track in proportion to increasing speed, then the legs come in under the body but should never cross. The line from the shoulders down through the leg should remain straight, although not necessarily perpendicular to the ground. Viewed from the rear, a Boxer's rump should not roll. The hind feet should 'dig in' and track relatively true with the front. Again, as speed increases, the normally broad rear track will become narrower.

Faults: Stilted or inefficient gait. Lack of smoothness.

CHARACTER AND TEMPERAMENT

These are of paramount importance in the Boxer. Instinctively a 'hearing' guard dog, his bearing is alert, dignified and self-assured. In the show ring, his behaviour should exhibit constrained animation. With family and friends, his temperament is fundamentally playful, yet patient and stoical with children. Deliberate and wary with strangers, he will exhibit curiosity but, most importantly, fearless courage if threatened. However, he responds promptly to friendly overtures honestly rendered. His intelligence, loyal affection and tractability to discipline make him a highly desirable companion.

Faults: Lack of dignity and alertness. Shyness.

DISQUALIFICATIONS

Boxers that are any colour other than fawn or brindle. Boxers with a total of white markings exceeding one-third of the entire coat.
Approved 1989.

INTERPRETATION OF THE STANDARD

Now that you have had a chance to digest the words which make up the Boxer Breed Standard, I will take you through the key elements in greater detail, highlighting areas of particular importance and attempting to provide clarification on some points which are not explicitly covered. I will go through this logically, starting with the head and moving through the various body parts, before considering movement and then ending up with the most important feature of all – the general appearance of the Boxer.

I have tried to make as much use of original illustrations as possible, because it is only by seeing examples 'in the flesh' that the verbal descriptions of particular points really begin to make any sense and, in doing this, I have made a real effort to come up with realistic examples. I have read far too many dog books (across many different breeds) where the examples of right and wrong have been so extreme that you would never encounter them in the modern show ring. I do not think that this helps anyone's understanding. In reality, the variations within a modern Boxer show entry are often not that great, and you must train your eye to pick up on the subtle differences between the exhibits. All of the examples which follow are based upon Boxers who have won well in the show ring, and so you will need to study them carefully to pick up on the various points which they illustrate. This chapter is certainly not meant as an 'idiot's guide'.

Head: muzzle, skull, mouth, eyes, ears and expression

We are directed to give special attention to the head, where one point seems very specific: the length of the muzzle (measured from the tip of the nose to the inside corner of the eye) makes up one-third of the total length of the head (measured from the occiput to the tip of the nose). It is important to emphasise that these measurements are from the tip of the nose and not from the front point of the muzzle. The problem with this 'specific' guidance is that it is only a ratio, which could logically be a 'long' or a 'short' one-third/two-thirds split. However, I believe that anything other than a medium-length head will not achieve an accurate fit in real life with several cross-checks contained in other parts of the Standard: with a long head it is usually difficult to obtain the desired tilt to the nose and the visible chin; while, on the other hand, it is hard to achieve good balance with the rest of the body if the head proportions are short, and the skull can often tend towards roundness in the shorter head. We have a medium-sized breed, so we therefore require a medium-sized head to achieve balance. We must remember that, although the Boxer head is at variance with the natural canine type, it should not appear extreme in any way.

The desired width of muzzle is more contentious. The UK Standard merely asks for the muzzle and skull to be balanced. In the past, some writers have taken this to mean that the muzzle should be the same width as the skull, but common sense has always told me that this cannot be the case. I can think of no adult Boxer head in any country that even comes close. I believe that the requirement in the American Standard for the muzzle to be two-thirds the width of the skull is correct, and this ratio fits all the excellent heads I have tried it out on. More importantly, in an outstanding recent article, Pat Heath of the Seefeld Boxers uncovered a copy of the *Deutsche Boxer Stammbuch* – the training manual for German judges – where this ratio is clearly stated. This gem of a book also tells us that the muzzle should be as deep as it is long.

You will see that all of these various measurements are incorporated into illustrations 1 and 5 and they make perfect sense. However, above anything else (and setting all talk of ratios to one side), the muzzle must look powerfully developed in all three dimensions and its power should derive from a good underlying bone structure, not just superficial plushing. While some padding is essential to fill out the space above the lower jaw, it must never be excessive; it should be confined to the muzzle area alone and the flews should be tidy. Linked to this, you should also make special note of the Standard's very specific statement that wrinkles should only appear on the dog's brow when he is alert. In some countries, there is a current trend towards very 'fleshy' heads. These are not correct and they are often associated with coarse skulls, whereas the actual requirement is for strong but clean cheeks with no unsightly bulges. I cannot abide 'cheeky' Boxers.

The correct jaw is an essential part of the muzzle formation and it is one example (there are many more throughout the Standard) where we can see that the form of our Boxer accurately follows its original function. As we saw in Chapter Two, the old Bullenbeissers were designed to leap on to prey and hang on until it was subdued and could be finished off by the hunter. A

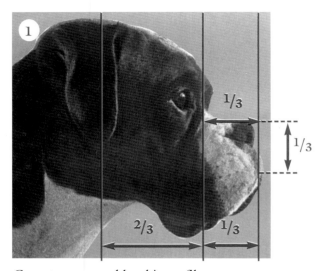

Correct, uncropped head in profile.

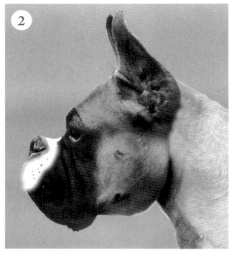

Correct, cropped head in profile.

This is not such a good head in profile, being rather flat and lacking in rise of skull. The muzzle is also a shade long, disrupting the ideal 1/3:2/3 ratio, and the nose lacks tilt.

HEAD PROPORTIONS

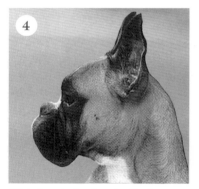

This head also has its faults. This Boxer has a good rise of skull, if a little exaggerated, but its muzzle is too short. The proportions of this head in profile are more 1/4: 3/4.

broad, solid top jaw coupled with an undershot lower jaw of maximum width is the most effective way of achieving this, because when the dog has a grip and gravity is naturally forcing his body weight downwards, the undershot jaw digs further into the prey giving the dog greater purchase. At the same time, a wide jaw prevents the dog from simply tearing out a mouthful of flesh as the prey rips itself free.

This is a good head showing the desired muzzle width – 2/3 that of the skull.

This head displays a good, clean skull, but the muzzle is a little light, being less than 2/3 the width of the skull.

A powerful muzzle, but the head is a shade strong in skull, which detracts from the ideal 2/3:1 balance.

The Boxer's design should allow him to grip firmly, not to cut. Sometimes at shows you hear disgruntled exhibitors pondering why their exhibit's bad mouth has let them down so badly. How many times have we heard the comment "I don't know why the judge minded, the dog can still eat." This objection really does miss the point completely – if the Boxer's bite is too level or two narrow, the dog would be in danger of slashing his prey and, if it is too undershot or wry, he would find difficulty in getting a firm grip in the first place. All these faults would make him unable to carry

MOUTH

Good mouth and correct jaw formation viewed in profile. Note how the dog is not excessively undershot – his upper incisors fit just behind his lower canines.

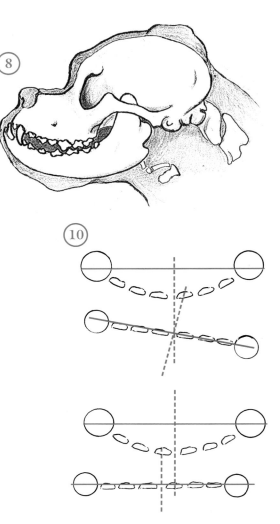
⑧

⑨

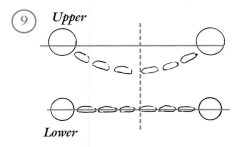

Upper

Lower

This is the same mouth depicted in diagrammatic form. Note the width of both upper and lower jaw.

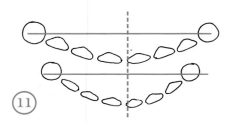

⑪

A narrow, rounded underjaw which is too undershot.

⑩

Two examples of wry jaws – a very serious failing.

out his original purpose effectively. The relevant illustrations (8-11) should help.

The naturally undershot jaw should also provide some finish to the head with a chin that is visible from the side as well as the front. Achieving this in conjunction with a wide straight mouth is one of the biggest challenges for the Boxer breeder. A lack of chin will mar the dog's expression, while too much chin (leaving the bottom teeth on view when the mouth is closed) will ruin the expression completely. You will have

noticed from the text of the Standard that there is only one disqualification recorded (that relating to colour), but my opinion is that having teeth on view is effectively treated in the ring as a disqualifying fault. It is a very serious failing.

The definite break (or 'stop') between the topline of the muzzle and the forehead is another essential breed characteristic, and so is the slight tilt to the end of the nose. This tilt allowed the dog to keep breathing while it was locked on to its prey. The

A beautiful head with excellent lip placement, evident chin, and the correct amount of padding and flew.

This head could do with a bit more chin and cleaner flews.

This dog displays too much chin, and you can see that he is very nearly showing his teeth as a result.

forehead itself should rise and then there is a further slight rise to the occiput. In profile, this all means that the head should look like a smaller square (the muzzle) attached to a larger square (the skull). It should never look flat. Look back at illustrations 1 and 2 and compare them with the dog shown in 3.

The expression of the breed is what endears the Boxer to most of us and I think this is described so well when the American Standard talks about eyes: "their mood-mirroring character, combined with the wrinkling of the forehead, gives the Boxer head its unique quality of expressiveness." What an accurate description this is, and

how well it emphasises the importance of the eye in giving correct Boxer expression! In brachycephalic or short-nosed breeds, the natural tendency is for forward-facing, round eyes (just check out the Breed Standard for the French Bulldog, Boston Terrier, Pekingese, Bulldog, Griffon and Pug if you have any doubts). The Boxer also requires direct, forward-facing eyes but – against the natural trend – they should most definitely not be round since this destroys the expression. Small or deep-set eyes are less common, but similarly undesirable.

Trying to describe the required shape of a Boxer eye is next to impossible, though it is

EYES

Correct eyes of excellent shape and size – truly mood-mirroring.

These eyes could do with being larger and less slanted.

HEAD STUDIES
A selection of beautiful Boxer heads.

Ch. Ashgate Able Seaman of Seefeld.
Photo: Teoh.

Ch. Norwatch Sunhawk Wanneroo.
Photo: Banks.

Walkon Uppa Gumtree.

Kate at Belire.

Ch. Ringside's Chanel.

Ch. Salgray's Black Tie.

akin to a diamond with rounded edges. Suffice to say that the bitch in illustration 15 has eyes to die for. As a matter of interest, and if the eyes are set correctly, an imaginary line joining up the two corners in each eye will be just about horizontal. Eye colour is another important consideration. Dark brown is what is required. Light eyes spoil the expression, while black eyes (just as serious a fault) make the dog look blank, rather stupid and sometimes menacing.

Ears are not generally problematic and, if they do happen to be set wrongly or if they are too big, it is normally instantly obvious due to the damaging effect on expression. In countries where they are not cropped, just make sure when judging that the natural ear is not disguising a rather thick skull.

I will bring this section to a close with two smaller points. It is essential that the head benefits from a black mask which will always encircle the eyes, but it should not extend so far as to create a sombre expression. The nose must also be black and we do like to see big nostrils, which became quite rare a few years back but now seem to be returning. Before moving on, take a long look at the lovely heads illustrated.

Neck and topline

Although it is somewhat contradictory, we want to see our Boxer's neck strong but flexible. We certainly do not want a swan-neck, since this would disturb the square outline of the breed, but nor do we want a stuffy, thick neck which always makes a Boxer look very common. A correct, sturdy neck of medium length, free from throatiness and with a distinct nape, gives the dog a degree of elegance and is highly desirable. You tend to find that this type of neck is usually present if the forehand of the dog is constructed correctly. In a well-made dog, the neck flows neatly into the withers but, in the case of a dog with straight shoulders and a short upper arm, the neck usually comes out at rather an upright angle and is often rather short. This will become much clearer to you when we come to the forehand illustrations. In the good examples (22 and 23) the necks are also correct.

So, the neck should flow neatly into the shoulders at the withers and this smooth line should then continue into a strong, broad and firm topline. The Standard asks for the topline to be slightly sloping, but how slight is slight? A complete lack of slope certainly ruins the characteristic Boxer

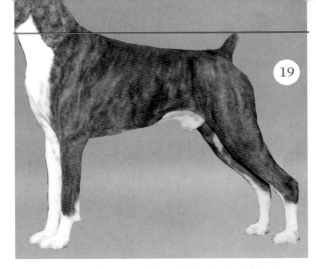

Correct smooth topline. The Standard allows for a slight slope to the croup, but this is a slope of the underlying bone (which can be felt) and not of the externally visible topline.

The Boxer topline should be "slightly sloping", but how slight is a slope? As a guide, a horizontal line drawn across from the withers should skim the top of a normally docked tail.

This is a slightly lumpy topline. It starts smoothly enough over the withers, but weakens in the area of the back and falls off slightly at the croup.

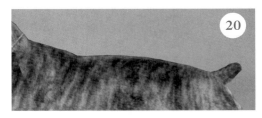

A topline showing a distinct roach before tailing off at the croup.

outline, but we do not want to fall into the trap of thinking the more slope, the better. Occasionally, exaggerated examples of this are seen in the ring. As a rule of thumb, an imaginary horizontal line drawn from the highest point of the withers should just skim the top of a normally docked tail. I am very well aware that this method depends on the length of dock and how the dog is positioned, but it is a good guide – have a look at illustration 19.

Forequarters and body proportions
Breeding a correct Boxer forehand is difficult, and the fact that there are so many poor forehands in the ring today proves it

beyond any reasonable doubt. This is especially disappointing because, if you get the forehand of the dog right, then so many other important virtues like neck, feet and topline seem to follow. As one famous American handler always used to say: "The Boxer hangs together from his shoulder."

So what should we be looking for? Most importantly, we want a long shoulder blade meeting a long upper arm at an angle of about 90 degrees. This means that the Boxer will then stand over his front legs and, when viewed from the side, you will see very evident forechest. Look at the bitch depicted in illustration 22 and the dog in illustration 23. These are two examples of lovely forehands and their bone structure will accord very closely to illustration 21. When you have studied these, compare them with the bitch shown in 24, who has a shorter upper arm which meets the shoulder blade at an angle greater than the desired 90 degrees. Because of this, she does not quite have the forechest we are looking for and you will see that she is not standing as well over her front legs. You will also see that her neck does not flow into her withers as neatly as it does in examples 22 and 23. However, compared to some Boxers that you see in the ring today, she is certainly not a bad example! Finally, have a look at illustration 25 where the upper arm and shoulder blade meet at less than a 90-degree angle. This is not as common a fault, but it is just as serious since it gives the Boxer an overdone, exaggerated forechest making him look a bit cloddy and lacking in elegance.

Moving round to look at our Boxer from the front, (illustrations 26-28) we want to see straight, parallel front legs. We also want to see a front which is smoothly covered with muscle. If the shoulder blade or upper arm are too short, the muscles will usually tend to be short and bunchy and you will see unsightly bulges over the shoulder. In these cases, the elbows will often stand proud, whereas in our ideal Boxer the elbows should neither stand away from nor be too tied into the chest wall. If the elbows do lie too close (in extreme cases the dog can look as though both its front legs come out of the same hole), it probably means that the Boxer is lacking width of ribcage which is a serious failing in a working dog. We do not want to see barrel ribs in a Boxer, but you should see a decent-sized oval shape in cross-section, with the

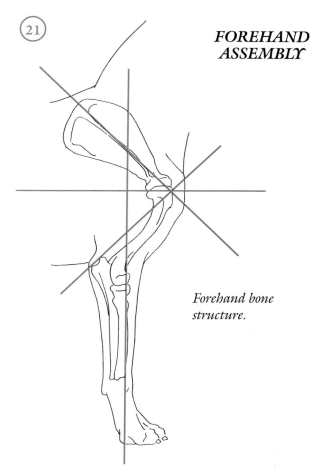

Forehand bone structure.

ribs extending well back down the body. This gives plenty of room for the body's powerhouse: the heart and lungs.

Turning to the overall body proportions, these are well defined in the Standard and give us our squarely-built dog. Have a look at illustration 29, which depicts a beautifully-made Boxer. A horizontal line drawn from the forechest to the rear of the upper thigh equals the height of the dog at the withers. The chest of the dog should extend down to the elbow and this point should be half the dog's height at the withers. If the chest does not extend as far as the elbow, the dog will look light and shelly but if it extends too far, the dog will look coarse. These are most important measurements. As well as my ideal example,

22

Correct forehand assembly in a bitch with correct length of neck flowing smoothly in at the withers, correct lay of shoulder and good length of upper arm. Note how this bitch stands over her front legs.

23

Correct forehand in a male.

24

This bitch is slightly short in upper arm. Note how this means that the forechest is not so evident, the neck does not flow into the shoulder as neatly, and the bitch cannot stand comfortably over her front legs.

25

This is an exaggerated and over-angulated front. It is slightly over-built and over-muscled giving a cloddy appearance, lacking in elegance. The over-angulation makes the dog stand too far over his front legs.

I have included another Boxer who is not quite square, for comparison purposes.

The only slight problem I have with these measurements, which check the Boxer for 'squareness', is that they can also work out correctly in dogs who are not perfectly angulated. Take a look at illustration 31 which shows a dog fitting the Standard's basic measurements, but you will see that he is not made half as well as our example shown in 29, being a little short in upper arm and not as good behind. To 'cross-check', I therefore suggest that you think of a third line. If you draw a tangent down the back of the dog's neck, it should extend to fall just inside the rear toes of a correctly-

The Breed Standard

FRONT VIEW

(26) A correct front: The legs are straight, there are no unsightly bulges over the shoulder, and the elbows are tidy. Note that there is sufficient width between the legs for the ribcage to house the body's essential organs. As in this case, good fronts are usually accompanied by good feet.

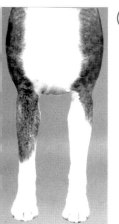

(27) This is also a very good front, with many of the attributes depicted in illustration 26, but it could probably do with a shade more width. In extreme cases, fronts can look as if both legs are coming out of the same hole.

(28) This front is incorrect. Note how the elbows stand away from the body, and look at the bunchy musculation over the shoulder. The feet are not perfect.

PROFILE

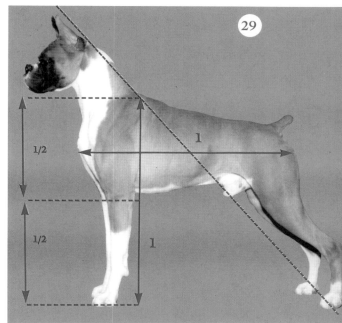

A very well-made Boxer male. The overall picture is one of harmony, with each constituent part following neatly into the next. Look at the body proportions and see how close they are to the Standard, giving the required square appearance.

BELOW: A very good Boxer, but slightly longer than tall, disturbing the required square appearance.

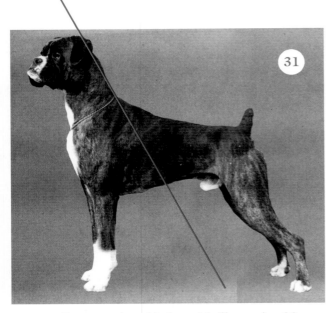

By comparing this dog with illustration 29, you can see how the tangent line drawn down the back of the neck can be a useful additional cross-check.

made and square Boxer. Have a look at where this line actually falls on my two examples. In the first (29), where the forehand is correct and the neck comes out at a smooth angle, my third line falls perfectly. However, in the second (31), the dog's slightly upright shoulder and consequent upright angle of neck, coupled with his poorer quarter, makes the line fall well short. I must emphasise that you should not get too 'hung up' on this third check, which does depend on how the dog is posed, but I have tried it on many photos of many Boxers and have found it to be a most useful tool.

Before we move on from the body, I will just emphasise the Standard's requirement for a curved underline. This has often been termed the 'line of beauty' since it is so important in giving the Boxer a touch of class. An otherwise excellent Boxer without this 'tuck-up' can seem very ordinary indeed.

Hindquarters

As a generalisation, modern Boxer hindquarters seem to be at a higher overall standard than forequarters, but one or two problems still creep in on a regular basis. This is unfortunate, because the hindquarters play such a vital role in providing the drive and power for our working dog. From the side, we want to see good broad upper and lower thighs sweeping down in a graceful curve to the hock joint. Your Boxer's quarters should give the impression of great strength without losing their smooth lines – we do not want our Boxers to look like Mr Universe. The hock joint should be well let down, i.e. the bone between the hock and the foot (the metatarsus) should be short, and this bone should stand almost upright when the dog is standing naturally. When posed, the knee joint (or stifle) is located immediately under the hip protuberance. These two points are clearly shown in illustration 32. However, as the precise location of the knee joint is not always immediately obvious from the outside, an easier trick is to imagine a plumbline dropped from just behind the rear thigh of the dog. In a properly angulated Boxer, where the stifle joint is correctly located, this plumbline will fall just in front of the dog's rear toes. Have a look at illustrations 33-35.

Moving round to the back of the Boxer, you want to see a straight line from the hock joint to the floor. You certainly do not want to see the hock joints turning in (termed cow-hocks, which are reasonably common) or out (which are less common). From this angle, you will also be able to appreciate the quality (or otherwise) of the smooth musculature on the dog's thighs

HINDQUARTERS

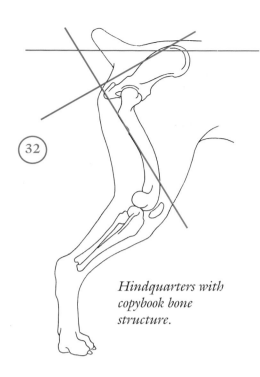

32

Hindquarters with copybook bone structure.

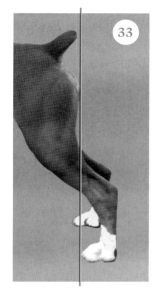

33

Well-angulated hindquarters with correct length of hock and knee placment. Note how the plumb-line dropped from behind the rump lands just in front of the rear toes. The upper and lower thighs are well-developed.

34

These quarters are over-angulated, and the plumb-line would drop well in front of the rear toes. This dog is also a shade long from the hock joint to the floor.

35

The basic angles of these hindquarters are not too far out, and the plumb-line would land correctly, but this dog is weak in upper and lower thigh,, and he lacks turn of stifle. He is also a shade exaggerated in hock.

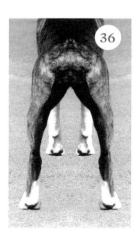

36

37

Excellent hindquarters viewed from slightly different angles. The musculation is well-developed, and the hocks are firm, turning neither in nor out.

38

This dog is a little cow-hocked, and his quarters lack quality musculation.

which you have already admired from the side. A good set of quarters viewed from behind is a lovely sight! Take a look at the two examples in illustrations 36 and 37 compared with the poorer specimen in 39.

One final point on hindquarters is to mention the Standard's comment that the tail is set high while the croup is slightly sloped. This strikes me as a bit of a contradiction and I actually believe that the allowance for the croup to slope refers to the underlying bone structure of the pelvis (have a look back at illustration 32), rather than anything visible on the outside.

Feet

I cannot add much to the Standard's explicit description of feet, except to say that poor feet are often an indicator that something more fundamental is wrong with the way the dog is put together. Poor construction often means that the dog's weight is unevenly distributed and the feet can therefore be caused to buckle under the strain. Bad feet are most unsightly and I often think that Boxers with poor feet are

FEET

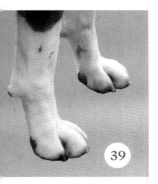

Good cat-like feet.

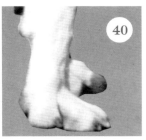

Poor, splayed feet. Poor feet are usually indicative of worse constructional faults above!

similar to cars with flat tyres. You will find that 39 and 40 are excellent illustrations of good and bad examples.

Colour and coat

The American Standard is much more helpful on this point and gives specific guidance on the distribution of white markings, which is lacking from the UK Standard. I must also draw your attention to the fact that the stripes on brindles must always be visible and the ground colour should be clear. The Standard actually gives a lot of leeway within the two permissible coat colours, but a Boxer should never look black. The coat itself should be short and Boxers with slightly longer, thicker coats can look common. We have already mentioned that it is this section of the Standard which contains the only disqualification, where Boxers more than one-third white (or any other colour except fawn or brindle) are unacceptable.

Size

This is defined quite clearly in the Standard, though the American version is worded in a much more tolerant way. Over recent years, the Americans have been widely criticised for the explicit allowances they make on size. However, I actually believe that they are right to do so, because our emphasis should be on balance. When you are assessing your own Boxers at home you can often be very surprised at their actual measurements, whereby a very well-made dog will invariably look smaller than a less well-made shorter dog. What we want is a medium-sized, square dog and as long as the exhibit before you falls into this category, I do not believe that we should worry unnecessarily about precise measurements. I hope we never see the day when anyone judges with a tape measure in their back pocket.

Gait

When the Boxer is moving away from you, what the judge is looking for is the hocks turning neither in nor out. We want to see the back feet digging in and the quarters showing real evidence that they are providing propulsion and not looking stilted. As the dog turns and starts coming back towards you, we are looking for straight front legs, neatly-held elbows and no paddling of the front feet. We also do not want to see any evidence, such as side-tracking, that the front legs are holding up the back legs or vice versa. When watching all of this, we must also bear in mind that as the speed of the dog's gait increases, it is permissible (and entirely natural) that the Boxer's legs converge towards his centre of gravity. Please remember that this does not mean that the legs bend, it does not mean that the dog single tracks, and it most definitely does not mean that the dog should move close at all speeds.

All books on canine movement agree that the desired angulation of the Boxer's forehand is the most effective for ensuring a ground-covering stride because it allows great reach. This should be immediately obvious as you watch the dog go in profile, when you should see the front legs extending well beyond the front of the dog's head (which will lower naturally when he gets into his stride).

Although the Boxer's forehand provides no propulsion on the move, this correct extension is vital since it allows the rear to provide optimum drive without interference. In saying this, you must recognise that for a Boxer to move well, the front and rear angulation has to be balanced because, if one half of the dog is built to move more efficiently than the other half, proper co-ordination will quickly be lost. What you want to see in profile is a smooth, easy action with no unnecessary or awkward movements. If, for example, the dog is too steep in shoulder, his front reach will be reduced and he will have to take shorter, more frequent steps to cover the same distance (in a type of movement more usually found in the Terrier Group). Even if his quarters are built to drive efficiently, they will not be able to do so because the front half of the dog will act as a limiter.

MOVEMENT

A good mover in profile displaying great reach and drive. In particular note how the feet remain close to the ground in an efficient gait.

TOP-QUALITY BOXER OUTLINES

TOP LEFT: Ch. Treceder's All That Jazz. Photo: Rinehart.

ABOVE: Ch. Seaside's Ewo's Surfbreaker. Photo: Booth.

LEFT: Ch. Jacquet's Millennium. Photo: Alverson.

BELOW LEFT: Ch. Sugarwood Didjano.

BELOW: Ch. Fletcher of Sunhawk Norwatch.

This type of Boxer may look startling on the move with legs flying in all directions, but it is far from correct and it will take him a lot of effort to get from A to B. We want a free and roomy stride. The movement should look effortless and the paws should never need to be lifted far off the ground, maximising efficiency.

A properly-made Boxer moving in profile is a pleasure to watch and, although it is difficult to capture in a photograph, illustration 41 gives you some idea of what I mean. Look at the fabulous extension of forehand, the evident drive from behind and see how close this dog's feet remain to the floor. You can also see that the topline of this Boxer has been maintained and the tail is carried high. If the topline of the Boxer is lost when it is moving, you must suspect constructional failings.

General Appearance and Overall Balance
A good Boxer will immediately catch your eye and he will give an impression of substance, yet at the same time retain his elegant, classy lines. As you can imagine, this is a most difficult balance to get right but, at first glance, you should not concern yourself with possible failings, just appreciate the qualities. Much of the initial impact will hopefully be conveyed by a well-balanced square outline which is so characteristic of the breed. If most of what we have been talking about in this chapter is correct, then the general appearance of the Boxer outline is arresting, especially when it is coupled with an outgoing temperament and the 'constrained animation' which is mentioned in the US Standard.

Have a look at the outstanding outlines featured in the photographs. Do not analyse them in minute detail, just stand back and appreciate the overall picture. These dogs exude Boxer type and create an initial impression which is very favourable.

These observations bring me neatly to the end of the chapter because I will finish off by reminding you of the order in which we should be making our assessment of the Boxer. First comes the general appearance, followed by consideration of overall balance. We then give special attention to the head, before we take a look at the individual body parts and movement. This tells us quite clearly that the Boxer should not be extreme and that, as breeders and judges, we must retain a strict sense of proportion. It is the overall appearance of our breed which comes first, and this must never be sacrificed in order to perfect a few small parts within the larger picture.

7 *THE SHOW RING*

The majority of people become involved in dog showing almost by accident. In most cases, families have located a breeder and have gone along to buy a companion puppy with no idea that a world of show dogs exists. They may have heard of Crufts or Westminster, but they will undoubtedly be surprised to find out that shows at many different levels take place every week, up and down the country, with well in excess of 10,000 dogs competing at the larger events.

Prospective owners tend to find this unknown world fascinating, especially when they can see winning animals at the breeders' kennels and when they hear about their puppy's famous ancestors. But in reality, they only came along looking for a puppy that would be a much-loved member of the family and, for many, this is as far as their interest in dogs will ever extend. They will enjoy getting their puppy's pedigree out to show friends and relatives all the Champions brightly marked in red ink, but they will probably never attend a show. However, every so often, a bit of gentle encouragement by the breeder to come along to a match night, or a chance remark

by someone later in the dog's life about how good-looking he is, may prompt owners to dip their toe into the world of showing.

It is a hobby which many people soon find thoroughly absorbing and almost addictive. I think that the main reason for this is because there is always something else just around the corner. You may not be winning particularly well now, but you have planned your next litter already and you just know that in 12 months' time you will be up there with the best. It is also a hobby that plays to your competitive instincts, and the excitement of battling for a place and seeing how results unfold differently on different days, maintains the interest week after week, year after year. But there is so much more to it than this, and you will find that, with such an absorbing common interest, friendships build up easily and, to most people, the social aspects of dog showing are almost as important as the dogs themselves.

However, before you all rush off into this utopian world where everything is perfect, you must be aware of the possible pitfalls too. In such a competitive hobby, there are bound to be the odd occasions when you need a thick skin to withstand throwaway comments from the graceless competitor; you need to have the time and the money to commit to your dogs and your hobby; you need the confidence to go into the ring and to make the best of your exhibit; and you need to be able to cope with the frequent knock-backs, as well as the occasional successes. How many of us have suffered a dog cutting his pad in the run-up to a show for which we had high hopes, a dog winning many prizes as a puppy then failing to come up to size, or a litter containing only plain dogs when we wanted a flashy bitch for the ring? We have all experienced these disappointments and many more besides but, in the world of show dogs, you need the temperament to come back fighting and waiting for the success around the next corner. In the back of every exhibitor's mind is the hope that, one day, they will have a Champion, be it their first or their next.

EARLY GROUNDWORK

The most important groundwork for you to do is to rear, nurture and socialise your Boxer correctly, since the one thing all top show dogs have in common is that each one is in the peak of physical and mental condition. You must also make certain that your Boxer is schooled to show himself off to best advantage.

We have already looked at the different methods of handling your Boxer and, in preparation for his show career, you need to consolidate this training at a very early age. You also need to make sure that your dog performs in a show environment. You often hear people saying "If only the judge could see him when I set him up at home!" Sadly,

ABOVE: Ch. Sirrocco's Kiss By The Book: Top Boxer in the USA.

BELOW: Correct rearing and show training is absolutely vital if you are going to stand a chance in the show ring. This puppy, the future Ch. C-Era's Dar's Deja Vu is in peak condition.

Photo: The Standard Image.

93

this is not possible and your dog must be used to giving his best performance where it matters most – in the ring. The easiest way of ensuring this is to go along to the monthly match nights and puppy walks that the breed clubs host. They usually take puppies from 12 weeks of age once their inoculations are complete. Here, you can practise with your puppy in a relaxed atmosphere and he can get used to concentrating, even when he is surrounded by other Boxers.

The person taking the class will go over your puppy for you, probably more than once. He will have a look in the puppy's mouth to get him used to this important discipline, and he will get you to move the dog just like you would do at a proper show. If you need it, you will also be able to ask for more help in getting your puppy to stand or seeking guidance on which method of handling suits you and your Boxer the best. I think these training classes are absolutely essential for the novice and seasoned exhibitor alike and, if you are a newcomer, please do have the confidence to ask questions and seek advice. This is what these club meetings are all about and you should find them invaluable.

Another part of your early groundwork should be to attend a couple of shows as a spectator. This will give you a much clearer idea of what to expect when you finally attend as an exhibitor. You will be able to watch how the other exhibitors show their dogs, how the judging procedure is carried out, and what arrangements there are for the dogs at the different types of show. At most shows you will also be able to buy show products from a much larger range than is usually available at local pet stores. It is much easier to get your bearings at a show when you do not have a dog in tow, and the less that is unusual on your first day as an exhibitor, the better.

ENTERING A SHOW
With very few exceptions, such as the small Exemption shows which are held as fundraising events, you will need to enter shows well in advance. The secretaries of organising societies will place advertisements in the main canine journals to let potential exhibitors know the date, judge, location and type of their shows. You can either telephone or send a stamped addressed envelope for a schedule of the event, which will contain full details of the rules and regulations covering the show, details of the different classes and an entry form. The schedule will also clearly show a closing date for entries and this must be met, or you will have your entries returned to you. However, you should not complete your entries too far in advance because, in calculating which class you are eligible for, you need to take account of all wins up to seven days before the entries close. We keep a special drawer for our schedules, separated into those already entered but yet to take place and those that have yet to close. In this way, we make sure that we do not miss anything.

The entry form is perfectly straight-forward to complete and you will not go wrong if you follow the instructions carefully. We always obtain a proof of posting certificate from the Post Office when we send our entries in, to ensure that we may still exhibit our dogs on the day of the show even if the entry form was lost in the post. This is a sensible precaution, as it will be accepted as proof by the Kennel Club if entries do go astray and any win you achieve on the day will stand. A historic cheque stub used to be evidence enough, but those days are gone.

When you are entering your dog, read the definitions carefully and make certain that you are going into the most appropriate class for you. In the UK, newcomers often fall into the trap of entering every class that they can. As a rule of thumb, this is not a good idea and you would be much better advised to stick to just the one unless there is more than one judge on the day, in which case you should give both a try. If you have a puppy, keep to the right class for your pup's age and, if you are out of puppy (i.e. over 12 months old), go for the easiest class you can see with the most restriction on previous winnings. This is likely to be Novice or Maiden. Classes such as Post Graduate, Limit and Open are best left until your dog has won his way out of everything else, and remember, you can always check with the show secretary if you need further guidance.

In the USA, the decision is made a little easier since you can only go in one class and there is a less confusing array to choose from, but the same rules apply – stick to the age classes and then graduate slowly up the scale.

There are several different types of show and these attract different types of exhibitor and a varying quality of entry. In the UK, Limited shows are at the lowest level. As their name indicates, entry to these shows is 'limited' to members of the show society, and they are usually comparatively small events. Big-winning dogs are not allowed to compete and the entry usually comes from the very local area. Open shows are next in line and these are far more common than Limited shows. Open shows are 'open' to anyone with a registered dog, but it is unusual to see Champion Boxers entered here, and owners who do bring their top winning Champions to these shows are usually considered a bit greedy. Although the Open show entry is also comparatively local, you can often see high-quality puppies and juniors competing. The bigger-winning adults are often saved by their owners for the Championship shows which are at the top of the UK show hierarchy. The competition at Championship shows is intense, since it is only here that you win awards that may eventually make your dog a Champion. Entries come from all over the country and you will normally see between 200 and 300 Boxers competing in the Championship show ring. There are nearly 40 such shows each year from Belfast to Crawley, Edinburgh to Paignton, and the seasoned exhibitor will be seen at nearly every one, trying to win one of the Challenge Certificates (CCs) that are on offer to the best male and the best female in breed. To win a CC (or a 'ticket', as they are more commonly known) in Boxers is no mean feat, since you have to beat the other 100-150 Boxers of the same sex on the day, and to become a Champion you need three CCs from three different judges. As you can imagine, the price of entering the different types of show varies enormously, from a couple of pounds up to nearly £20 per dog for the large all-breed events. As I have said before, campaigning a dog seriously is not a cheap hobby!

While the three types of show are the main building bricks of the UK show scene, there is a distinct difference between the show that is run by an all-breed society and the one that is run by one of the 15 UK breed clubs. It is fair to say that the breed club show is very close to the heart of the UK Boxer exhibitor and they invariably get very good entries indeed, even at Open and Limited level. While an all-breed Open show may struggle to get 20 entries, a breed Open show will normally get well over 100. One reason for this is that the breed shows are often combined with a 'Puppy Sweepstake' that is judged by a separate judge and which gives you two bites at the cherry on the same day if you have a puppy to show.

I have read many arguments in many different books as to which show is the best for a newcomer to start at, assuming that they have already got some experience under their belt at the match nights I talked about earlier. There is consensus that a Championship show is not a good place to begin (and I would agree) but, aside from this, opinion seems to be divided. My own strongly held belief is that a breed club Open show is by far the best option as your first show. The clubs always make an effort to find a hall that is big enough for the job, the judges are normally experienced with the breed (but not so experienced that they have forgotten what it was like to be a newcomer), there is little time pressure so you can safely assume that you will be given a second chance if your puppy lets you down when you first move him and, from an educational point of view, the better dogs, the better judging and the more experienced owners will usually be there. However, the most important thing with any show you may choose is that you turn up, have a go, and talk to people. This is the way to learn.

In the USA the lowest level of show is the Match, which is organised either by a breed club or by an all-breeds society. Champions are not allowed to compete and no awards are made towards the title of Champion. These are often sociable events and they are good training grounds. Next, we have the All Breed Championship show that is the backbone of the US show scene. The US has many more Championship Shows than we do in the UK, and the entries are usually smaller and more localised. This is a function of geography as much as anything else. All the dogs which are not Champions compete for the award of Winners Dog and Winners Bitch, which gives you some points towards the title of Champion. Then the Winners go forward to the Best of Breed Class to meet all the Champion entries, and it is from here that an ultimate Best of Breed is declared.

You will notice that, unlike the UK, dogs in America do not have to beat all of the established Champions when they are trying to pick up their points. In addition to the All Breed shows there are also the Specialty shows run by the breed clubs. To win at a specialty is a great honour and highly prized because these can be absolutely huge occasions. To give you some idea, the National Specialty in Boxers (run by the American Boxer Club) takes place over five days, and can attract up to 900 entries from all over the continent and beyond. To win at the Nationals is the ultimate accolade and, in my opinion, the event is the greatest Boxer show on earth. An annual trip to the Nationals is the best holiday you can have.

To make your dog into a Champion in the USA you need to win 15 points, and you are awarded between one and five points each time you go Winners of your sex. The precise number depends upon the size of entry actually present on the day.

An overview of Westminster Kennel Club, America's most prestigious show.

However, if your dog is to become a Champion, not only do you need to win these 15 points but, within this, your dog must also have at least two 'Majors' under different judges and these are defined as three, four or five point wins. The number of points available at each show depends upon the breed and its location, with the American Kennel Club constantly trying to equalise the points available from breed to breed and from area to area.

BEFORE YOU LEAVE HOME
Show days are busy days and this is especially true if you are new to the game and need time to get your bearings. Because of this, I always think that it is as well to do as much as you can at your leisure before the big day dawns. About a week before the show, we start adding a very small amount of cod-liver oil to the dinners of our show dogs as we find that this noticeably improves the sheen on their coats. Then in the run-up to the show we give the dogs a bath. There are many pet shampoos on the market, but I have to say that we have most success with normal human beauty

products, finished off with a high-quality conditioner. These also tend to be considerably cheaper than the fancier canine brands! We never bath the dogs on the day immediately before a show, as it takes 24 hours for the coat to settle down and there are few things more frustrating than trying to disguise a scurfy coat at a show.

Boxers are an incredibly easy breed to prepare for the ring, but on the evening before the show you will need to spend half an hour with a stripping comb, some scissors, a pair of electric clippers, a grooming glove and an assistant, in order to put the finishing touches to your dog. Boxers should have a lovely clean-cut outline, and you can enhance this enormously by tidying up some edges before a show. I hope that the photos will assist greatly in your understanding of this section. Start with the stripping comb and

A small amount of cod-liver oil added to your Boxer's diet will give his coat added sheen. Int. Ch. Kitwe Out of the Blue's dark brindle and white jacket looks magnificent in the sunlight.

SHOW PREPARATION

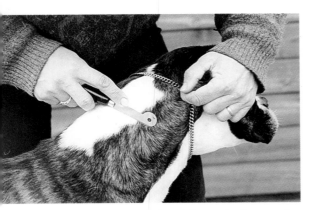

Remove excess hair with a stripping comb.

Carefully trim your Boxer's underline with a pair of electric clippers.

You must also shave off the long whiskers on your Boxer's face.

LEFT: Trim the 'feathers' down the back of the legs into a neat straight line. Start off by using a pair of scissors then carefully add the finishing touches with the clippers.

RIGHT: Use the scissors to trim the long hairs at the end of the tail.

run it down the dog's neck, then use it down the back legs. You do need to be firm with the comb to have the desired effect of removing excess hair, but you must not be too firm as this will damage the skin.

When you have finished with the comb, use the grooming glove briskly over the whole body to remove any remaining loose hair. You can now get the clippers out, and a human beard-trimmer will do the job perfectly well if you cannot immediately locate professional pet clippers. Run the clippers carefully along the dogs underline, paying particular attention to the tuck-up and the area behind the dog's elbows. It is sometimes helpful to lift the dog up by his front feet when you are doing this. When you have finished, move your attention to the dog's face and give him a shave, carefully removing all his whiskers and eyebrows. You will also find that Boxers often have hairs growing out of 'beauty spots' on the side of their heads and under their chins. These need to be removed as well. I have to say that, even when we are doing this for the first time, our dogs take to the noise and the sensation of the clippers remarkably well.

When you have tidied up the face, take your scissors and trim the 'feathers' on the back of the legs into a neat straight line. You should also trim around the end of the tail to smarten things up. Once you have trimmed the longer hairs of the back end with the scissors, you can take the clippers again and tidy up the lines even more. The end result is sharper and neater, and I think it makes a tremendous difference to the look of the dog in the ring. In the USA, the trimming of show Boxers has developed into much more of an art than the simple process I have described here, but this is

undoubtedly best left to the professional handler. My basic method will achieve 90 per cent of the end result with a lot less effort and much less chance of making a complete hash of things, but, if you are attempting any of this for the first time, the best advice must be to practise on an older dog first or try it out on your show dog when he does not have a show for a couple of weeks.

As well as trimming and cleaning your dog, you should also get your showbag ready beforehand. This is what we keep in ours: a blanket for the dog to sleep on during the day; a chain and collar with which to attach him to his bench if it is a benched show; a water bowl; a towel to rub him down before he goes into the ring; some approved coat preparation to add final lustre to his jacket; our chosen tidbits or small toys to keep his attention in the ring; a show lead and fine choke chain; a ring clip to hold the exhibit number; some nappy sacks to enable us to clean up after our dogs; antiseptic cream, antihistamine cream and some eyedrops (just in case!); a mobile phone to keep in touch with home; the schedule for the show and exhibitors' passes if there are any; scissors and the stripping comb for any last-minute touching up; and a plant sprayer filled with water to keep the dog cool in the ring on a hot day. You should also consider taking a crate if the show is not benched, to make the day more comfortable for your dogs, while folding chairs may make life easier for you (though you might find that you soon need a pack-horse as well to carry it all!).

As a final part of your preparation, decide what you are going to wear. There is no point in being outlandish. The main criteria are that the colour of your outfit should complement your dog (there is no point wearing dark colours if you have a dark brindle dog as this will mask his outline completely); you must be able to move your dog effectively (no high heels or flapping skirts); and you should have easily accessible pockets where you can store your bait and toys. You will do your dog a lot of favours if you follow these simple rules. The American professional handlers have all of this off to a T. Just have a look at some of the photos throughout this book – smart jackets and trousers in sensible colours, flat shoes and big pockets.

AT A SHOW

The most important thing is to arrive in good time, so plan your journey carefully and overestimate the time that it will take you. Being late and having to rush your Boxer from pillar to post to get into the ring on time is not the best way to make him give a first-class performance. When you arrive at the show, buy a catalogue and locate the ring where Boxers will be judged. Catalogues can seem expensive these days but I view them as essential reference documents, since they contain the breeding details of all the dogs entered and they will enable you to build up an idea of the type of dogs you like and the breeding behind them. You should also immediately check that your entry is correctly detailed in the catalogue. If it is not, have a word with the show secretary who will be able to check it against your entry form.

As long as you are not in the first class of the day, make sure that you have a good look at how the judge is going through his entry so that you will know what is expected of you when it is your turn – how he is moving the dogs and where he likes

them set up for examination. You should also check the ring for any potential pitfalls. By this, I mean that you should avoid getting squeezed out of sight in a corner, you should certainly find a piece of level ground as nothing looks worse than a Boxer standing downhill, and you should avoid a location where your dog is pointing straight at the sun since this can make reasonable eye colour look poor, and poor eye colour look positively disastrous, as the dark pupils narrow in the strong light and the lighter colour of the iris takes over!

As your class approaches, get your dog out to apply the finishing touches to him, and make sure you have got your ring number clearly displayed or that you know what the number is if they are being given out in the ring. Allow your dog to spend a penny before you take him into the class and, above all, keep calm. Nerves are transmitted down the lead at the speed of light and your dog needs reassurance from you, not the reverse.

When you go into the ring at the start of the class, it is best to position yourself about halfway through so that you can get settled before your turn. This also gives you time to calm down after you have done your bit before the all-important closing minutes of a class when the final decisions are made. Be confident in your manner. If it is your first time in the show ring, you can be sure that no-one else will know, so there is no need to be self-conscious. There are enough poor handlers in the UK show ring to keep you company, if your first efforts are not quite as professional as you might have hoped for.

Do remember to keep your dog looking good whenever the judge might be looking. This does not mean that he has to be on his toes throughout the class, but the best handlers always keep one eye on the judge so that their charge is only ever seen looking at his best. While the class is being judged you may also like to try and shelter your Boxer from the sun with your shadow and, although he can obviously satisfy his natural nosiness as you are waiting for all the other class entries to be examined, you should not let him tire himself unnecessarily – a good Boxer head always looks so much better if the dog is not panting. On top of everything else that you have to do, please, above all, remember that nothing you do when showing your dog should be off-putting to the other exhibits: squeaking a toy, throwing liver all over the ring or letting your dog sniff another one being set up is not going to win you many friends. Actually, these are all simple rules that you will already have picked up at your club training sessions.

If you are lucky enough to win, try to look pleased as opposed to surprised – you should take it in your professional stride. As a winner in the UK, the judge will write a few words about your dog and this 'critique' will appear in the weekly dog papers, telling you why your dog won on the day. Finally, when you get home after a successful show, remember to keep an accurate record of your wins as they will affect which classes you are eligible to enter in the future.

SPORTSMANSHIP

We are all involved in what must be the most subjective sport in the world and, if you listened to all the ringside gossip that goes on after a show, you would hear 101 different reasons why a particular dog won under a particular judge. These range from the particular favourite "it was bound to win, it's sired by his dog", to the equally frequent "they always travel together". On top of these old chestnuts, you can add a multitude of more obscure and even more scurrilous reasons that are trotted out by disgruntled exhibitors week in, week out. However, in my experience, cases of really dishonest or incompetent judging (yes, they do exist!) are so few and far between that they are best forgotten and written off to experience. I believe that 99 times out of 100, the judge goes into the ring, judges to the best of his ability, concentrates intently and tries as hard as he can to put up what he considers to be the best dogs on the day, regardless of external influences. If you accept this and do not get involved with the more racy gossip, I can assure you that you will have a much happier showing career, and class placings will make more sense to you than any of the whingers and whiners.

The most important thing for you to remember is that the description of an ideal Boxer that we looked at in the chapter on the Breed Standard is mere words on a page and the perfect Boxer has yet to be born, so the ideal will always be open to some personal interpretation by judges of the breed. I am sure that we have all played the party game where you have to describe an object to people in another room without the use of anything but words and trying to get them to draw it accurately. Even with the simplest of objects and lots of words, the end result is never very satisfactory and, if more than one team is playing, the differences between the drawings can be enormous. This is how it is with a Breed Standard – the words conjure up slightly different pictures to different judges and this is why the same dog will never win all the time. Be gracious both in victory and defeat and, even if you do not particularly like the Boxer which has won, you can still be pleased for the owners – you will expect them to be pleased for you when you are celebrating. A few kind words from fellow exhibitors always help to make a good win into a great one. In the UK, we can be pleased that sportsmanship remains at a good level and, when you do make up your first Champion, you will be amazed at the number of congratulations cards you get and who they come from!

Be prepared to believe that judging is honest, be pleased when others win, make the most of it when you win, keep dog showing in perspective among life's other priorities – and you will enjoy your showing to the full.

OPPORTUNITIES TO LEARN

The best way to learn is by going to shows and building up your experience. You can learn a tremendous amount by watching judging closely, by watching other handlers at work, by talking to other exhibitors, by seeing how other breeders are going about their own breeding programmes, and by following the end results in the ring. It is for this reason that it always depresses me to see newer exhibitors turning up at a

show, maybe showing in the first class of the day, and then going home immediately if they do not win! I know that it is not always possible to hang around, due to commitments at home, but I have always looked upon shows as full days out and we always stay to the end. To leave early is to miss an opportunity.

Building up your knowledge by hands-on experience is naturally a gradual process, and the history of most exhibitors who are successful in the long run tends to go something like this. They start off showing a Boxer who is really not quite good enough and, although they soon realise this, they recognise that their first dog is giving them some fun and is providing them with good handling practice until something better comes along. The fact that they have persevered in the ring will also stand them in good stead when they approach a breeder, since the breeder will know that any puppy they let go will be campaigned properly and that the exhibitor will make a reasonable job of it. Once the exhibitor has something better, then he may have his first litter, keep something better again, and so on. It is in this way that you build up the quality of your stock, and patience is a great virtue.

8 *JUDGING BOXERS*

The judge of any breed, at any level, has a fundamental role to play in keeping that breed true to the precise description laid down in the Breed Standard. In fact, I would argue that judges are the most important individuals in the world of pedigree dogs, more important even than the breeders themselves – though I am aware that this is something of a 'chicken and egg' argument, since without breeders there would obviously be no dogs to judge. However, I do feel most strongly that, if clear guidance on correct type and soundness is not given by judges in their placings and awards, a breed runs the very real danger of splitting off into many different factions with personal preferences and exaggerations becoming rife. True type quickly evaporates when it is not consistently rewarded in the ring and to support this argument, it is clear that the strongest breeds are those where the judging population is able to maintain a reasonably cohesive collective responsibility towards the type of animal required by the Standard.

I think it was for these reasons that one of the most famous lady judges in British Boxer history, now sadly no longer with us, once said that judges can make or mar a breed. I agree with her wholeheartedly and I believe that, with such a vital role, a strong breed needs individuals who do judge and do not merely place the dogs brought before them. Almost anyone can place dogs, but it takes a very seasoned eye to judge them against each other and, more importantly, against the ideal laid down in the Standard. An experienced Boxer judge

Ch. Roamaro Scotch Mist of Winuwuk who is being handled by the author, winning Best in Show. Scotch Mist is runner-up to the breed record holder and she has won more than any other brindle Boxer. Photo: Jackson.

will be able to assess the exhibits objectively and, after judging, will be able to comment on the current areas of concern to which he feels that breeders should direct their immediate efforts. As long as the message from the judges is consistent, this is the way in which they can keep the breed on track and in which correct type and conformation can be preserved and prized.

There is no doubt that judging is much more difficult than it looks; it is not obligatory and would-be judges should approach the task with the gravity it deserves.

STEWARDING

The steward's job is to make sure that the ring is run smoothly for the judge and that all the necessary paperwork is dealt with in a professional manner. It is also a good way for up-and-coming judges to get a feel for being in the ring, and it provides them with an opportunity to watch the work of an experienced judge at close quarters. In some countries, it is a required part of the apprenticeship for trainee judges, and there is certainly some logic in this. So, if you do have a desire to judge, it is a good idea to get in some initial stewarding experience first. The all-breed societies are usually crying out for good stewards, and their secretaries would be delighted to hear from volunteers, though it is obviously sensible to start off at a show where there are two stewards per ring. This will allow you to learn the ropes from a more experienced colleague.

As a steward you should be quietly efficient and unobtrusive. It is the judge's ring, not yours. There are many important aspects to the job, but one that seems to escape most stewards is the announcement of the placings. The ringsiders want to be able to mark up their catalogues accurately, so call out the winners' numbers at the end of the class loudly and clearly. Stewards who do this quickly become very popular!

Good stewarding is really appreciated by judges, as it makes their life so much easier, allowing them to concentrate 100 per cent on the dogs; so, in return for your efforts, judges will never mind discussing the reasons behind their placings with you over lunch or after the judging is complete. Some of my most interesting and educational discussions have been with judges I have stewarded for.

QUALITIES AND QUALIFICATIONS
Number one on the best list of judges' qualities I have ever seen was "good eyesight". I am sure that the writer had her tongue in her cheek, but it is a serious point. Judging is physically and mentally draining – just ask anyone who has judged a big Championship show entry at the height of a summer heatwave – and so you need the physical capacity and stamina to carry out the task, giving as much undivided attention to the last dog of the day as the first, even though your feet are killing you and your back is about to break.

You must have a detailed working knowledge of the Breed Standard and a very thorough understanding of canine anatomy. This will allow you to give absolute and correct reasons for your decisions when you have completed your judging. However, even the most physically fit candidates, with the most comprehensive knowledge of the Standard ever known, will never make good judges unless they have the personality for the job. Judges need to operate at the highest level of

Anne Rogers Clark, one of the world's greatest all-breed judges, awards a Best in Show to Ch. Heldenbrand's Jet Breaker who is being presented by Gary Steele.

Photo: Callea.

honesty and integrity, and you need the ability to banish all external influences from your mind – you are in the ring simply to find the best Boxers on the day. Any thoughts of a dog's past wins, settling old scores, trying to improve your own chances for future shows, courting popularity, spreading the awards around, judging on pedigree, worrying about how certain people will react to your judging, putting up friends (or deliberately putting them down!), avoiding the dog that 'everyone' said you were going to do, repaying favours, etc. etc., are all forms of dishonesty and they have no place in the show ring. Anyway, why make life difficult for yourself? Your sole task of finding the best Boxers on the day is hard enough, and I will never know how people find time to think about this other endless list of do's and don'ts.

You will need to be decisive and to act with absolute authority, but this does not mean that you have to be overbearing. Exhibitors always appreciate showing under a judge who looks like they are enjoying

themselves, who remembers a few common courtesies, and who puts the handlers at their ease. This is a difficult balance to strike.

In terms of actual qualifications to judge, Kennel Clubs in different countries work very hard to maintain the standard of Championship show judging by imposing certain minimum criteria. If you do have a long-term desire to judge the breed, then you should get in touch with your local breed club secretary to establish the current local procedures. In some countries, formal examinations are required, but in others, such as the UK, the system is based solely upon an individual's showing and judging experience. In the UK, the Boxer Breed Council operates a comprehensive system of judging lists beneath Championship show level in an attempt to ensure that all judges meet minimum standards. As an example, you should not expect to judge Boxers at even the smallest show until you have been showing successfully for at least six years and, once you do start judging Boxers at these small shows, you will need to judge a certain number of classes over a further four-year period before you will be considered competent to judge a breed show. You will then need to get a couple of breed shows under your belt before you can think about a Championship show. This process is designed to allow individuals to build up a thorough understanding of the breed over a period of time and it has a lot of merit.

Perhaps the only point it does not really consider is how successful the aspiring judge has been with his own stock in the ring. If they are ever going to breed good show stock, exhibitors have to judge their own Boxers continually and develop a keen eye for quality and correct type. If a breeder never manages to put good Boxers into the show ring, then it is questionable whether they have the eye for a good dog that is so essential in a judge. There is no doubt that the judges who ultimately command the most respect are the ones who have first proved their ability as exhibitors.

INVITATIONS

The cardinal rule here is that you must wait to be asked. Few people are less respected in the show world than those who go around touting for judging appointments.

When an appointment does come your way, you should firstly satisfy yourself that you are qualified and that your name is on the correct judging list to allow you to accept. There is no stigma attached to declining invitations and, if you are uncomfortable in any way, you should politely turn the offer down.

If you do decide to proceed, you should read the invitation carefully and check it for any stipulations laid down by the organising society. It is common practice that you will be asked to refrain from judging the breed within a certain time period and geographical radius from the show you have been asked to judge. This is as much for your benefit as the Society's, since you want as good an entry as possible and this will not be helped if you have recently judged in the same area – the dogs you did not place are hardly likely to come back under you for a second bashing. In similar vein, you should limit your ringside comments in the run-up to a judging appointment, since you do not want such throwaway comments to affect the numbers that come under you.

You should reply to the offer letter promptly, agreeing to all the conditions, and you should keep a copy of all the correspondence. The secretary will

Boxer breeder and judge Stephanie Abraham awards Best of Winners at a Boxer Specialty to Ch. Kreyon's Let's Dance. Christine Baum is handling.

Photo: Kernan.

complete the judging contract by sending you a confirmatory letter on receipt of your acceptance, and then a few weeks before the show you will be sent a schedule, usually indicating the numbers in your entry and any final arrangements.

PROCEDURE

First things first: do dress sensibly. Although you must dress smartly, it is not a beauty pageant and your clothes must be suited to the job: comfortable, worn-in shoes; nothing that will flap in the dogs' faces when you are going over them (ties are always a problem and need restraint); no large or clanking jewellery; and no strong perfume or aftershave. You must also make sure that you have suitable wet-weather gear, just in case. There are one or two pieces of equipment that you should take: a pen; a pad or a small Dictaphone, so that you can take notes on your winners to help you with your subsequent critique; and, as it saves you making silly noises all day, I also like to take a small squeaky toy to help me check the dogs' expressions.

You should aim to arrive in very good time. You can always sit down out of the way and have a coffee when you get there to kill an hour, but it is unforgivable to cause the organising society and the exhibitors problems by being late. As a secretary, I can tell you that I am always very glad to see a judge arrive and, if they are not there at least half an hour before they are due in the ring, I start having kittens.

About ten minutes before judging begins, make your way to the ring and introduce yourself to the stewards. Discuss with them how you would like the ring to operate, make the best use of all available space,

decide how you are going to move the dogs and ensure that everything can be seen from the ringside – this is a spectator sport after all. If you do bump into anyone you know before you start judging, it is obviously best not to have a full-blown conversation, but it is equally daft to pretend that you have never met them before and head for cover. A simple "hello" will do nicely.

You will obviously not see a catalogue before you judge, but have a look at the judging book and see how the entry is split up. This will help you to pace yourself. Although we all have our own individual judging methods, I think that consistency is a most desirable characteristic when judging. This means that the exhibits know exactly what will be expected of them and it ensures that you give everyone equal consideration, which is most important as each exhibit has paid the same amount of money for your opinion.

Personally, I like to see the class come into the ring and I will always walk around to get an initial impression of the Boxers on show. Once you start doing this and have passed the first dog, get him to set up for examination in the middle of the ring so that he is ready for you when you have finished your overview. In examining a Boxer, be direct and firm in your approach. Never swoop on to a dog, never approach it first from behind and never be uncertain in your touch. This does not mean that judges ought to be rough, but Boxers appreciate a confident hand.

I always take a long hard look at the overall picture first – as the Standard says "in judging the Boxer, first consideration is given to general appearance." In this respect, I am always reminded of Philip Stockmann's report which was printed in the American dog press after he had judged at Westminster way back in the 1930s when he wrote: "General appearance shall dominate over all other qualifications."

Once you have gained this overall view, go round to the front of the dog and check its expression and its front, before getting your hands on the head to check the bone structure of the muzzle and the bite. When you have done this, run your hands over the dog's forehand and shoulders, which should be clean and free from bulges. You should also place a hand between his front legs where the chest should fill your hand, indicating plenty of heartroom. Continue your hands-on examination down the dog's back to see that he is well ribbed up and not too long in loin. If it is a male dog, you will now need to check that he has two testicles. Finally, I like to feel the quality of the musculation on the dog's quarters and the width of second thigh.

When you have finished with your hands, walk round to the back of the dog to check for straightness of the hind legs and firm hocks and then, on your way back round, pause at the 'three-quarters' view from behind, as this is an excellent vantage point to look at the dog's forehand assembly. If the dog is out at elbow, this is one of the best places to see it. Then, before asking the dog to move, have a final look at overall balance with the benefit of your closer examination stored in your brain. It is at this stage that you may want to check a specific point again.

How you get the dog to move will depend upon the size and layout of your ring, but the most important thing is that you check the movement in profile as well as straight up and down and that you move all the dogs in the same pattern. It is when

viewing the dog in profile that you get to see him in the raw, without the benefit of a good handler pushing and pulling him into position. If the ring is big enough to allow the dog to move in a large triangle, great, but if you have to change your judge's position to make sure that you can see the dog in profile, so be it.

Before moving the dog, indicate to the next exhibitor in line that you would like him to set up his dog ready so that, when you have watched the previous exhibit move, you can turn round and start smoothly on the next. This saves a lot of time in a large entry.

When you have gone over all the dogs, and if the class is large, it may be sensible to separate the 'men from the boys' by making an initial cut. When doing this, I always shortlist the dogs that I would consider 'very good' or better under a grading system of judging, so the number I bring out will depend upon the overall quality of the class. By bringing a dog into the final cut, you are rewarding good type and you are making it clear that the Boxer was worthy of further consideration. You are also making life easier for yourself as you approach your final decisions.

When you are making your final evaluation, recognise the virtues of the individual Boxers first and then take into account any failings. You must not approach judging the other way around, because a dog with very few faults but no virtues is of very little use to anyone. You should also take care not to dither in the final analysis. The best piece of judging advice I was ever given was to make sure that you were doing something when you were thinking – move the dogs round, have another look at expressions – but do not

While Christine Baum, Harriett Campbell and Eleanor Linderholm-Wood were awarding the American title to Ch. Cayman's Black Bart...

(Photo: Nutting)

... Jenny Townshend, Helen Banks and Joy Malcolm made Ch. Roamaro Scotch Mist of Winuwuk their winner, with Ch. Huttonvale High Command of Seacrest best opposite sex.

Photo: Banks.

stand there staring into space; this will do nothing to inspire confidence! If you really are stuck on one particular decision with two dogs of equal quality, I always settle the debate by asking myself which one I would be happiest with in my home kennel. I know that many other judges also use this simple trick.

There is much to think about when you are judging, but most of it is common

sense: do not hold conversations with any of the exhibitors; do not address any exhibitor by his Christian name; do make an extra-special mental note of the first dog in the class, so that you know when you have completed your hands-on examinations; and please make sure that your facial expressions do not give away too many of your thought processes. Other things are more personal preference than anything else, but I do like to see judges create a bit of interest when they come to the final awards. This does not mean playing to the ringside, or making someone think that they have a major win in the bag when they have not, but it does mean shortlisting, it does mean taking second looks when they are required, and it does mean making awards clearly and decisively so that everyone knows who has won and when they have won it.

Proper judging also means the ability to convey your findings on the day in a written critique of the main winners. I know that this is not done all over the world but, in the UK, exhibitors appreciate judges who write sensible, balanced and factual critiques which are tactful, not toxic. In my view, you should consider the critique as a requirement when you accept a judging appointment. To help you write it, please do take notes on your winning dogs.

The chances are that you will remember your principal winners in great detail, but it is better to be safe than sorry. We have certainly had brindle dogs described as reds in written reports, which does rather dent one's confidence in the rest of what the judge has to say.

RECORDS
In this day and age, it is essential that you maintain clear and comprehensive records of your judging assignments. This will enable you to complete nomination forms and judging CVs accurately in the future. You should also make sure that your records contain a note of all the absentees, as judging qualifications now depend increasingly on numbers of dogs actually judged, rather than the number entered. It is certainly sensible to retain your judging book and the marked-up catalogue from every show that you have judged.

9 PRINCIPLES OF BREEDING

There are many reasons why owners of a Boxer bitch decide that they would like to breed from her. Some of these reasons are good and some are not. So first of all, let us just check your motivation for wanting a litter. The belief that having some puppies would be good for the bitch is one myth that can be dispelled immediately, so please do not use this one as an excuse, because veterinary evidence is stacked against you. On the other hand, you may think that having paid a significant sum of money for your Boxer, you would like to see some return on your investment. Again, this is not a good place to start and you can bet your bottom dollar that, if this is your reason for having a litter, it will be a disaster. Yes, on occasion, some people do seem to make a quick buck from pedigree dogs. But, if you do it properly, you will find that the stud fee, the vet's fees, correct feeding and rearing and the advertising of puppies you cannot sell (not to mention the time and effort you need to put into a litter), will make it a very marginal exercise at best.

Remember, responsible breeders have years of experience in rearing litters and they make it look simple, but raising Boxer puppies is no easy task and I could quote many instances where owners, having tried it once, never want all of that hassle again. In my opinion, the only valid reason for wanting to breed is when you have a good-natured, well-bred bitch of some quality and you want to keep one of her puppies yourself. If this is your motivation, then your whole approach to breeding a litter becomes entirely positive. You choose the stud dog extremely carefully, you do not care how many puppies the bitch has – as long as there is one for you – you lavish all the care you can on the pups because you are going to end up with one of them, and you are in no rush to sell the litter too early because you appreciate the extra time to decide which one you are going to keep.

In saying this, please do note that my valid reasoning can apply as much to a companion litter owned by a single Boxer-owning family as it does to the top show kennel in the country. Some breeders would have you believe that breeding should be left entirely to the 'experts'. This is not true and, as long as your motivation is correct, there is no reason why you should not breed from your bitch. The show kennels do not have a monopoly. All I would say is that you must approach the task with your eyes open to the potential difficulties and prepare carefully.

TIMING AND PREPARATION

Your bitch puppy will probably come into season for the first time between eight and twelve months of age, though it is not unusual for it to be even later than this. From then on, you will find that she comes in at regular intervals of between six months and a year. It is very difficult to predict precisely what this cycle will be, as every bitch seems to be different these days. Although nature is best left to its own devices, we have found that a course of Vitamin E can prove quite effective at chivvying our bitches along if they are proving remarkably slow at coming in.

As a bitch approaches her seasons, you will notice that her vulva begins to show slight puffiness and, soon after, she will begin to show 'colour' (i.e. you will see a bloodstained discharge coming from her vulva). As Boxers are a very clean breed, you may not always notice this immediately and so, when we have a feeling that one of our bitches is coming in, we check for colour every day by dabbing her vulva with a white sheet of kitchen paper. About nine or ten days after you first spot the colour, you will notice that it has changed from bright red to a very light pink. This is a sign that your bitch is almost ready to be mated. Other signs are that her vulva will usually firm up a little and she will often 'stand' and switch her tail to one side when you stroke her thighs. You hear all sorts of stories about bitches being ready for mating on the most unusual days of their seasons, but in

During your bitch's season her vulva will swell. When she is nearly ready to be mated you will probably find that she will 'stand' and switch her tail to one side when you stroke her hindquarters.

Boxers this is very much the exception rather than the rule and we successfully mate the majority of our bitches on their 11th and 13th days. If you wish to be more technical about it, your vet can take regular blood tests from very early on in a bitch's season to identify the point of ovulation, but this always strikes me as an expensive way to identify a time that, in our breed, is usually very obvious. However, talking of vets, you should definitely get your vet to check your bitch over well before she comes into season, to advise you whether, in his opinion, she is suitable to be bred from. This is a very sensible precaution.

Boxers are a slow-maturing breed and you should certainly not consider breeding from your bitch until she is at least 18 months old and, before you mate her, you should make absolutely certain that the timing of the puppies will suit any other commitments that you have. You must take into account the fact that the gestation period is two months and two days and this will be followed by at least eight weeks when you will be tied to the house looking after the puppies – longer if you are keeping one. If you do have a completely free choice, I personally prefer litters born away from the height of summer since, although you can turn heat on, it is difficult to turn it off and, as we will see in the next chapter, temperature control is a most important part of puppy rearing. From choice, I would also avoid litters where the resulting puppies will need to be sold either during the school summer holidays or in the run-up to Christmas, as the market always tends to be a bit dead and you may end up stuck with puppies for a couple of weeks. This is a double whammy, since youngsters always settle into new homes better if they can go young. You will also find that feeding a large number of growing puppies quickly becomes very expensive.

Well in advance of the mating, you should also establish where you are going to whelp the bitch. This needs to be a quiet, warm, secluded location ideally in (or attached to) the house. You also need to buy (or make) yourself a decent whelping box, an infra-red heat lamp and a supply of specially designed whelping blankets. None of this is cheap. The whelping box should be just over one metre square, with pig rails around the perimeter, to prevent the bitch squashing puppies between her and the walls of the box, and it should have a let-down ramp on one side so that the puppies can get out when they are a few weeks old.

Your final piece of preparation must be to ensure that you have made arrangements to get your puppies docked. At the time of writing, docking is not illegal in the UK but it must be carried out by a vet. The breeder of your docked pup should be able to put you in touch with a vet who is willing to carry out this simple procedure, or you could get in touch with the Council of Docked Breeds. American breeders should experience no difficulty in locating a suitable vet.

LINE-BREEDING, IN-BREEDING AND OUTCROSSING

When we looked at buying a show puppy, I spoke of the merits of buying a Boxer which was reasonably line-bred and said that this would provide you with a solid foundation for the future. Line-breeding is a technique very widely used by dog breeders in an attempt to consolidate virtues in their line while simultaneously trying to minimise any faults. Essentially, it means mating family lines together to fix a certain type. It involves matings such as half-brother to half-sister, grand-daughter to grand-sire, cousin to cousin, and so forth. In this way, breeders are striving to retain the virtues of the family group while simultaneously bringing in new blood and hoping to correct failings by the involvement of different 'in-laws'. You will have to excuse the layman's terminology, but it gives you the idea.

In-breeding is really nothing more than an extension of line-breeding, as it still

Ch. Blueprint Beern Skittles at Walkon (above) was mated to his aunt to produce Ch. Walkon Crocodiledun Dee (below).
Look carefully at the two photographs and note the very close resemblance between these very good Boxer males. Line-breeding is a useful tool, enabling breeders to fix a certain type into their lines.

involves the mating of family members, but it is one stage closer, with the two parties being much more closely related – maybe brother to sister or father to daughter. Some kennels have done a degree of in-breeding over the years, the best example being the famous Wardrobes kennel of Constance and Wilson Wiley. Tight in-breeding obviously worked for them since they still hold the record as the top winning UK Boxer kennel of all time. This method of breeding can certainly be a more direct route towards fixing type much more quickly than line-breeding, but it also entails great risks. Virtues will undoubtedly be consolidated but so will any faults that are lurking in the background, especially those which seem to be inherited in a simple recessive fashion, such as light eyes and excessively undershot jaws.

It also strikes me that, if it is carried out for too long, an in-breeding programme can very soon result in the loss of temperament and a lack of bone. It also closes down your options, for, unlike a line-breeding programme where you have slightly different bloodlines with which to work, following an in-breeding programme will give you fewer and fewer to work with and very soon you may find that you have such a tightly-bred line that even the most dominant outcross introduced would face an uphill battle to have much influence. My own view is that this type of breeding can only be carried out by breeders who know the full background to their pedigrees intimately, and I would be very reluctant to take it to excess. However, I have the greatest respect for those breeders who do make it work and it is a fact that some of the most dominant Boxer sires in history, both here and, especially, in the US, have resulted from in-bred matings.

Outcrossing is the mating of two dogs who have no (or very remote) common family ancestry. Every breeder has to outcross from time to time to bring in some hybrid vigour to his lines, though you will usually find that careful breeders will then often mate the resulting puppies back to their own stock in the second generation to ensure that the qualities of their line are preserved, together with the plus points gained from the outcross. The result of an outcross litter is undoubtedly harder to predict, but it is often no bad idea if one parent is of outstanding quality and very tightly-bred. If this is the case and you mate such a Boxer to another with a reasonably open pedigree, you hope to get more of the dominant, outstanding parent. Many successful show Boxers have been bred in this way.

Our own philosophy has been to follow a line-breeding programme with the judicious use of dominant, good-producing outcrosses from time to time. We are certainly not alone in this. Most successful UK kennels have done the same, and we all make sure that we know the strengths and weaknesses of our own stock so that we only double up on virtues, never on faults, since a line-breeding programme based on poor-quality stock is a recipe for immediate disaster. There is no point having six lines back to a certain Boxer if that dog had bright orange eyes and spent his entire life cowering behind the sofa.

THE BROOD BITCH

Your brood bitch and her immediate family should be of good temperament and free from any outstanding faults. This does not necessarily mean that she has to be a show dog – many of our best Champions have been born to quite ordinary mothers. For a brood bitch, 'ordinary' is fine but 'faulty' is to be avoided at all costs. If you start out with a foundation bitch who has several glaring faults, the real likelihood is that you will need a significant number of future

BROOD BITCHES

It is not necessarily true that Champions always make the best mothers, but Ch. Romaro Scotch Mist of Winuwuk (right) and Ch. Faerdorn Knobs And Knockers (page 116) have proved to be outstanding brood bitches.

Photo: Dalton

Ch. Roamaro Scotch Mist of Winuwuk (top) produced Ch. Winuwuk Play Misty for Me (right).

generations to eradicate them from your lines. Some faults in particular, such as wide fronts and poor toplines, can prove especially intractable and, even when you finally think that you have them licked, they have a nasty habit of popping up again and slapping you round the face. It is so much better to start with either a very good or a very 'standard' bitch, and doing so will save you a lot of time and a lot of heartache in the long run.

When you do start to think about mating your bitch, take a very close look at her and

ABOVE: Ch. Faerdorn Knobs and Knockers (photo: Hartley) produced...

BELOW: ...Ch. Faerdorn Head Over Heels to Santonoaks. Photo: Trafford.

evaluate her very carefully. What do you like about her and what would you like to improve? If you do not yet feel qualified to do this, ask her breeder for his opinion, because this assessment of her is vital when you come to choose a stud dog.

Before the mating, your bitch should be in peak physical condition, well muscled and not too fat. In terms of paperwork, she must be registered in your name at your national Kennel Club and you must comply with any breeding restrictions imposed by the breeder when you bought her.

The one thing a brood bitch is not is a puppy machine, and few things depress me more than looking through the Kennel

Club Breed Record Supplement to see bitches having litter after litter. There can, of course, be no hard-and-fast rules as to how many litters a bitch should have, since it depends so much on how many puppies she has and whether she is a good mother. In some instances, taking a second litter would be a criminal offence, while in other cases bitches have the puppies quickly, take to motherhood easily and seem to thrive on it. My personal view is that three litters is quite enough and I would never mate a bitch after her seventh birthday. Outside of these parameters, I would need convincing but, if your motivation in breeding is merely to keep a puppy from the mating, I doubt that you will even get to three litters, let alone any more! You also need to make absolutely sure that your bitch is rested between litters. I believe that a 12-month gap should be a minimum.

THE STUD DOG
A dog who is able to complete the physical act of mating a bitch does not automatically qualify for the title of 'stud dog'. To me, a stud dog is an animal of proven worth to the breed who has consistently demonstrated his ability to pass on qualities to his progeny from a variety of differently bred brood bitches. This also means that an outstanding show dog does not necessarily make a brilliant stud dog, since the dog himself may be a 'one-off' and, if he does not have the ability to replicate his finer points, then he is of limited value to the breed. In my opinion, a worthwhile stud is likely to be of good show ring quality, have a reasonably tight pedigree, and come from a family of high-class Boxers (if a stud dog has shocking brothers or sisters then he is probably best avoided). The best stud dogs

we have seen in the breed fall within my definition.

If you are convinced that you have a dog who meets these criteria, then he is probably worth a try, but monitor his early litters carefully and, if the end results are disappointing, leave him alone and try elsewhere. As I said with the brood bitch, there is no point spending a lot of time and effort on a Boxer who is never going to produce the goods for you. This is especially true with a dog, because you can pursue much better options with the best dogs in the country standing at public stud.

When you are starting a dog off it is as well to try him on a calm, proven bitch, who is not going to do anything silly while the young pretender learns his trade. You should also never try to handle a dog at stud for the first time without the supervision of someone who is experienced in these matters. Dogs vary enormously in their maturity, but we usually try a young dog at about 12 months, which often coincides with the time when they start cocking their legs. The urge to mate is quite natural and we do not often encounter difficulties but, if you do have a slow starter, there are a couple of tricks you can employ. Stand in front of the bitch, lift her front feet off the floor and walk away from the dog. For some reason this always seems to make the stud dog climb on and, when he has the message, you will often find that you can lower the bitch back to the floor and he will stay mounted. The penny soon drops that he has to thrust as well. If you get nowhere the first time, do not despair and, if possible, use the second trick. Put the young dog in a crate in the mating room and let him watch while you mate his possible bride to another, experienced stud.

STUD DOGS
Both these dogs were outstanding winners in the American show ring and they went on to prove their worth as Sires of Merit.

ABOVE: Ch. Wagner's Wilvirday Famous Amos, and his son...

BELOW: ...Ch. Berena's Tribute to Fa-Fa.

This sounds daft but it works, and next time he will not want to miss out again!

Choosing a stud dog for your bitch is a long process and it involves careful preparation, both watching at the ringside and at home with pedigrees. If you have studied your potential brood carefully and objectively, you will be looking for a dog who will not spoil her good points and will, at the same time, improve other points. If you are conscious of a particular improvement that you are seeking, look for a dog who consistently produces this quality in his offspring. Some dogs are dominant for particular virtues. What you must never do is try to 'cancel out' faults, for example by mating a hollow-chested bitch to a wide-fronted dog in the hope that you will obtain something in the middle. All you will get is a split litter, with some taking after mother, some after father and none correct. What you ought to do is mate the bitch to a dog with an outstanding front, with good fronts behind him, and who has also proved his ability to pass this very desirable virtue on to his children.

In your search, you should make a mental note of which lines seem to click well together. You may notice that several bitches of similar breeding to yours have been successfully mated to a particular dog with winning puppies now in the ring. Also note those studs who may not be in the ring any more, but who are throwing puppies of a type you like and, remember, if you fancy a young dog – have a look who he is by and think about going back to the sire before you are tempted by the youngster. In your search for a stud, trying to match virtues and faults is the most important exercise but, once you have come up with a few possibilities, then have a look

at the pedigrees. It is beneficial if there is some family tie-up on good-quality ancestors, but, if this is not possible, go for a dog who is tightly bred himself. You may need help at this stage because you will not know the dogs in the background, so, again, ask your bitch's breeder for advice. Listen to this advice, as it will be based on experience, but, at the end of the day, she is your bitch and it is your decision.

When you are researching possibilities, please do not ask for stud cards from every top kennel in the land, in the belief that this will win you instant recognition and popularity in the breed. It will not. Believe it or not, stud dog owners do talk to each other and it is amazing how we all get to find out when an individual has asked for 25 different stud cards and only has one bitch to mate! Speak to the owners of the couple of dogs on your shortlist and ask for a pedigree. You should also discuss with them the breeding of your bitch and the points you are trying to improve, but, as always, it remains your decision. Take every bit of advice you can, consider it all and then make up your own mind.

Choosing a stud dog is never easy and nothing is guaranteed. However, I can guarantee that the best stud for your bitch is unlikely to be your own dog; he is unlikely to be owned by a friend of yours; he is unlikely to live around the corner; and he is unlikely to have the cheapest stud fee. You are doing yourself and the breed no favours if you plump for one of these easy options merely out of convenience.

THE MATING
In an ideal world, you will have selected the stud you wish to use well in advance of your bitch's season. Also, you will already

have spoken to the dog's owner to let him know that you will be bringing her along when she next comes in, though please do not make this sort of verbal commitment if you think you might change your mind!

On the first day that you see colour, telephone immediately and confirm a booking. Having spent a considerable amount of time making your decision, you do not want to leave it and run the risk that the dog will be booked. Some stud owners will ask you to obtain a certification from your vet that your bitch is free from infection, which involves a simple swab test. Some bitch owners like to put them on a five-day course of antibiotics immediately they come in, just to be on the safe side, but I have to say that we do none of this unless a bitch has missed previously.

At the time you book the stud, confirm terms with the owner. The commonly accepted terms of a stud contract are as follows: the bitch travels to the dog; you pay the stud fee immediately after a successful mating; you are only entitled to one mating and you are paying for the mating, not the guarantee of puppies; in return, you are entitled to assume that the dog has not served another bitch within the previous 48 hours, and you will be given a Kennel Club certificate signed by the stud dog's owner to enable you to register the litter.

I believe that these are your basic 'rights', but you will find Boxer stud owners an accommodating lot and you may find that they are prepared to vary these terms in your favour. Most will be happy to agree that you can have a free repeat if your bitch misses, some may be prepared to take a puppy in lieu of the stud fee, and most will be happy to let you have a second mating

within 48 hours of the first. The issue of a second mating is interesting. If you have had one proper mating there is no good reason why you should need another, but psychologically it makes you think that you are increasing your bitch's chances of conception. I think you will find that most breeders like two matings when they use an outside dog, so it is not unreasonable to expect them to offer the same service when bitches visit their dogs. The important thing with all these terms is that you both understand them clearly before the day of mating.

On the appointed day, please turn up on time and do not bring the whole family. A stud is a business appointment, not a social outing. It is sensible not to feed your bitch beforehand and to allow her to spend a penny shortly before you arrive at the stud dog's home. You should also make sure that she is wearing a snugly fitting collar to enable you to control her during the mating. When you arrive at the kennels, leave the bitch in the car and announce yourself. If you bring your bitch to the gate immediately, you will probably start a frenzy among the dogs and their barking will do nothing to settle her nerves. The stud dog owner will control the mating and you should follow his instructions carefully.

Thankfully, Boxer matings are usually uncomplicated, natural affairs and two people present are quite sufficient (one to work the dog and one to hold the bitch). We do all of our studs in a small room which is carpeted to stop the dogs slipping. We put the stud dog in a crate in the room and then bring the bitch in and let her off the lead. Once she has settled into her surroundings, we let the dog out and the two will normally engage in some foreplay,

MATING

1. As the dog mounts the bitch, make sure that you have a firm hold on each side of the bitch's collar. You should apply pressure downwards to give you maximum control without strangulation.

2. As the dog swells up inside the bitch, the stud dog handler must keep the dog and bitch steady.

3. Once the pair are tied, the dog should be eased off the bitch's back.

4. It is quite natural for the male to 'turn', leaving him back to back with the bitch until the tie subsides.

Photos: Banks.

with the dog courting the bitch. You may find that she is not immediately responsive, but if she is ready, she will soon start 'standing' firmly for the dog. When he starts to mount her put your two thumbs through the underside of her collar on each side, applying pressure downwards and guide her head firmly forward with your forearms. This stops her from turning round and having a snap at the dog when he penetrates her, and it stops you from strangling her, since the collar pressure is on the back of her neck and not on her windpipe.

Some bitches do not seem to notice when they are being mated, others squirm a bit when the dog initially enters, but, if they are going to struggle, the majority do so when the dog is inside and starts to swell. This wriggling is usually fairly minor, but you need to be ready for it. It is most important that bitches are kept steady throughout the mating.

On the other side of things, the stud dog handler will occasionally need to give the dog a guiding hand and sometimes, if the bitch is quite small behind, a dab of lubricating jelly will help. When the dog does penetrate he will start to pump furiously and, during this phase, the bulb of his penis engorges with blood and the dog will 'tie' to the bitch. The average tie lasts about 20 minutes, though it can go on for an hour or more. During this time the dog often wants to 'turn' so that the two parties will usually end up back to back. This is nature's way of protecting the couple because, during this time in the wild, the dogs would be very vulnerable, so it is sensible that they should both be looking in opposite directions for possible attackers.

Textbooks will tell you that it is the bitch who determines the tie, but I simply do not believe this. At the moment, we have three stud dogs: one ties for 10 minutes, one for 20 and the other for 25. This time stays the same for every mating that they do, and common sense tells me that it is the dog who is in control. When the tie does subside the dog will drop out of the bitch and, although his penis will still be extended, he will very soon tidy himself up and it will return to its sheath. If it does not, seek veterinary advice immediately. The bitch may be returned to the car. Any thought that she needs to be dangled upside down by her back legs, or needs to have her vulva dabbed with ice to make it contract and ensure that none of the sperm can escape, strikes me as absolutely laughable.

The dog's sperm was ejaculated during the first few minutes of the mating and, during the tie, it has been sent well on its way by lots of prostate fluid. You are not going to improve chances of conception by using these racier old wives' tales and the bitch will think that you have taken temporary leave of your senses!

If things do not proceed smoothly, the most likely explanation is that the bitch is not ready. A bitch who does not feel she is ready will not hesitate to let you know and there is no point forcing her; not only is this cruel, but it is also completely futile as the bitch is telling you quite clearly that she is not ovulating. On other occasions, the bitch may stand quite happily but the dog may slip out soon after he has penetrated. This is another sure sign that the bitch is not quite ready. In any of these cases leave her 24 hours and then try again. If this second try is worse than the first, then the chances are that she has gone over, and you will have to wait until next time. One other possible explanation is that the bitch may be a little over-protective of her owner and, occasionally, we get the bitch who does nothing but sit at her owner's feet and grumble every time the dog approaches. In these cases, we tend to get the owner to leave the room and we conduct the mating ourselves. It is amazing how often the bitch opens up when she has no-one to protect, and successful matings can usually be achieved. Once the bitch is tied, the owner can obviously come back in to confirm that the mating has taken place.

If you have had a 'slip' mating (i.e. with no tie), it is unlikely that the bitch will conceive and, although we all know of cases where a mating without a tie has resulted in puppies, these are very few and far between.

A tie is a pretty good indicator that the bitch is ready and that the mechanics of the mating have been carried out satisfactorily. If you have had a slip mating, you must not consider using an alternative stud dog on that season.

Talking of alternatives, in the unlikely event that the stud dog will not perform on the day, do not allow yourself to be talked into one of the kennel's other dogs unless you really are totally happy about using him. If you are not sure, it would be much better to wait until your bitch's next season rather than make a spur-of-the-moment decision that you may live to regret.

Finally, please do not get too emotionally involved with the whole procedure. Some owners seem to find it all quite upsetting, thinking that their bitches have some kind of innocent, virginal quality and that a stud almost equates to rape. This is not the case – it is the most natural act in the world and most bitches positively enjoy the experience.

COLOUR

In Boxers this is a straightforward subject. If you mate a red to a red, all of the coloured puppies will be red. Two brindles mated together, or the combination of a red and a brindle, will usually result in a mixed litter. However, some brindles are termed 'dominant brindle', which means that they do not carry the red gene and can therefore never produce a red puppy. Of course, this does not mean that all of their grandchildren will be brindle, since a proportion of the bitches that go to a dominant brindle will obviously carry the red gene.

I have noticed over the years that it tends to be the darker brindles who are more likely to be dominant, but this is certainly not a hard-and-fast rule. What is indisputable is that some of our best-producing dogs and bitches of the last decade have been dominant brindle. This should concern no-one, for, as I said at the start of the book, your task is to breed good Boxers and colour is a minor consideration. However, I do think that stud dog owners should make it quite clear when people use their dogs whether they are dominant or not.

The other issue on colour is that of white Boxers. In the UK and USA show rings, it is desirable for Boxers to have flashy white markings (though this is governed by fashion, not by the Standard!). Dogs who have these markings carry a white gene and, when you mate two dogs who carry the white gene together, simple genetics tells you that 25 per cent of their offspring will be white. You know from our discussions on the Standard that whites cannot be shown, nor can they be bred from, and we consider the ethics surrounding white puppies in the next chapter. From a breeding point of view, it is merely important to remember that neither the stud dog nor the brood bitch is 'responsible' for the number of whites in a litter – they both carry the gene so they have an exactly equal responsibility.

Just like the dominant brindle who does not carry a red gene and therefore cannot produce red puppies, some dogs do not carry the white gene and therefore cannot produce white puppies. Current thinking is that Boxers who do not have white feet (or who have a very small amount just on the toes) are unlikely to carry the white gene. It is for this reason that some stud dogs can be guaranteed not to sire whites.

Both of these good producers were dominant brindle.

ABOVE: *Ch. Tyegarth Famous Grouse sired 17 English Champions.*
Photo: Pearce.

LEFT: *Dolf The Buhe Farm of Marbelton was one of the most influential stud dogs to be imported into the UK from Continental Europe.*

HEREDITARY CONDITIONS

Boxers have remained a remarkably healthy breed. This is due in no small part to the continuous efforts of responsible breeders and their willingness to face up to one or two problems that have arisen over the years.

Progressive Axonopathy (PA) is a breed-specific disease of the nervous system which reared its head in the UK in the early 1980s. PA causes the degeneration of the nervous system and manifests itself at an early age, with affected Boxers going off their hind legs. It is a most distressing condition and affected Boxers need to be put to sleep. Thankfully, the mode of inheritance was quickly identified as a simple recessive, and this allowed known carriers and lines to be isolated and excluded from breeding programmes. Swift collective action was taken by breeders under the guidance of the Boxer Breed Council and, as far back as 1982, its geneticist, Dr Bruce Cattanach, wrote: "The PA saga has been brief. With careful breeding, the disease as a serious problem could become a thing of the past in a few years." Thankfully, due to the focus provided by the Breed Council and Dr Cattanach, this was how matters turned out and reported cases of PA totalled less than 100. This was a considerable achievement. Today, I do not believe that any breeder is working with lines that have a known carrier within five generations, but it does no harm to check with the breeder when you come to purchase a puppy or select a stud dog.

Heart murmurs have recently been recognised as a problem within the breed. It must be emphasised that these do not affect health in the great majority (95 per cent) of dogs, but those few Boxers with very loud murmurs may be subject to fainting and there may even be sudden death. Aortic stenosis is the heart condition most commonly associated with these heart murmurs. It must be stressed that minor 'flow' murmurs are commonly found in young Boxer puppies, as in other breeds, but most disappear by about 16 weeks of age. Even if they do persist, there may be no cause for alarm if they are quiet, since such genuine 'flow' murmurs are not associated with heart disease in the adult. However, the incidence of Boxers with severe aortic stenosis has increased in recent years, though numbers remain very low in relation to the numbers of dogs bred.

Nevertheless, to rectify the situation the UK Boxer Breed Council developed a system of testing based upon simple stethoscopic examination by cardiologists and a breeding control scheme was established. In simple terms, reputable breeders now have all of their breeding stock heart-tested and dogs with loud murmurs are not used. When using a dog at stud, you should ask for details of the heart score and, when buying a puppy, you should make sure that the breeder is participating in the control scheme. At the time of writing, dogs with a score of 0 or 1 (on a scale of 0-6), and those who have been established as clinically normal by Doppler examination, are considered suitable for breeding. The mode of inheritance of this condition is not yet entirely clear, but it is indisputable that the lower-scoring Boxers do tend to produce lower-scoring offspring.

As a responsible breeder, you may seek further details of both these conditions from the secretary of the UK Boxer Breed Council. However, it is important to recognise that it is entirely positive that both conditions have been confronted head-on by breeders and, because of this, incidences are being kept to a minimum.

In the United States, Progressive Axonopathy was never a problem and no American lines were ever implicated. However, heart testing is now commonplace, and, similarly to the UK, American breeders are adopting a wholly responsible attitude. The American Boxer Club has its own health and research advisers and details of the current schemes may be obtained from this Club.

AFFIXES
If you are intent on building up a strain of Boxers of your own, you may wish to approach your national Kennel Club with a view to registering your own kennel name. This will be your unique 'trademark', and you will place it at the front of the name of every puppy that you breed. In selecting affixes, different people use different techniques. For example, some people use amalgamations of their names such as Mary Hambleton's Marbelton kennel or Sue and Les Drinkwater's Sulez, while others use place names like Pat Heath's Seefeld Boxers. Whatever you choose, make it snappy and memorable, and make sure you like it – because you will probably have it for a long time!

10 PREGNANCY, WHELPING AND REARING

After you have successfully got your bitch mated there is very little to do for the next five weeks and you should not change your bitch's routine in any way. She can be exercised as normal and you should keep her on her usual rations.

You will naturally be very keen to know whether she has 'taken' or not, and this can be a frustrating period because you spend a lot of time convincing yourself that she either is or is not carrying pups. There are one or two signs that you can look out for. You may notice that the bitch's vulva does not seem to have reduced to the size it was before she came into season; she may appear to be taking extra care of herself; her nipples may be just that little bit more prominent and, as time goes by, you may think that you notice her filling up in body, especially just after she has eaten.

Your vet may be able to give you a better idea, when she is four weeks gone, by feeling her abdomen, as puppies can often be felt at this age as a row of round balls about three centimetres large. However, we have been fooled on many occasions and all these indicators are difficult, if not impossible, to detect accurately. The best advice is to be patient because, after five weeks have passed, your bitch should be very obviously in whelp and, if it is not obvious by five and a half weeks, you can begin to assume that she has missed. You can also assume that she has missed if she blows up far too early – a bitch who looks in whelp a couple of weeks after mating is almost certainly having a false pregnancy.

THE NEXT FOUR WEEKS

For the last four weeks of her pregnancy, when it is clear that your bitch has taken, you should still keep her on the same quantity of food as normal, but you should increase the ratio of protein to carbohydrate in her diet; in other words give her more meat and less biscuit. At this stage, we also start to give the expectant mother two raspberry-leaf tablets twice a day and we keep this up until a few days after she has had the pups. These tablets make for easier whelping and limit the retention of afterbirths. As your bitch is now getting noticeably bigger she will be looking after herself, but do play your part in stopping her from doing silly things like jumping into cars.

125

This bitch is five and a half weeks in whelp. Note how her nipples are enlarged and she is beginning to fill in behind the ribcage.

This is the same bitch pictured a few days before her six puppies were born.

During the final week of pregnancy, we add a calcium and multi-vitamin powder to her diet, in the quantity recommended, but we still keep her rations the same and we still make sure that she gets a limited amount of exercise. It is most important that pregnant bitches are not allowed to get fat and flabby. They need to be well-fed, not overfed.

During this last week you also need to get your whelping kit together. In the last chapter, I got you to prepare your whelping box, lamp and washable synthetic fleecy blankets (best known as Vetbed). You now need the following: copious quantities of newspaper; a clock; some paper and a pen; a digital veterinary thermometer; some specially-formulated milk powder; a pair of surgical scissors; towels; a bowl of disinfectant solution; a premature-baby feeding-bottle; a hot-water bottle; a small cardboard box; glucose powder; and your vet's telephone number, displayed prominently. When you are looking up your vet's number it is a good idea to give him a call to warn him that you are expecting a litter imminently.

You need to set up your whelping room a week or so before the event, so that your bitch can get accustomed to these strange surroundings. We like to move our bitches across into their whelping quarters a good few days before they are due.

THE ONSET OF WHELPING

It is difficult to say exactly when a bitch will start to whelp because, although the gestation period is officially 63 days, it is not unknown for bitches to be early or late and, if you have had a couple of matings, you do not know when the bitch actually conceived. You also have the added complication that sperm can live inside the bitch for a couple of days, which may put your calculations even further out. Suffice to say that the puppies are usually born at any time between the 57th and 72nd day after the first mating.

The most reliable method of monitoring progress is to take your bitch's temperature regularly, by inserting the thermometer gently into her anus. The normal temperature for a dog is 38.5C (101.3F) and, when her temperature drops back to

When it is almost time for your bitch to whelp, she will start 'nesting'. You should ensure that there is plenty of newspaper in her box.

about 36C (95F), you can reasonably assume that she will whelp within 24 hours (please note that her temperature will return to normal before she actually starts whelping and will probably hover slightly above normal for the following couple of days). When you have noticed this characteristic drop in temperature, you will probably also find that the bitch goes off her food, will soon start to become restless and to puff and pant, and she will begin nesting. This involves scratching up her bedding, so you should ensure that there is plenty of newspaper in her box. This really is the first stage of whelping and, for about six to twelve hours, the bitch's uterus is beginning to contract without any abdominal contractions.

THE BIRTH

Although the onset of whelping may occur during the day, it can almost be guaranteed that the actual birth will take place at night. I once read an interesting theory that, if the bitch was mated before 11 a.m., you could be certain of daytime puppies but we tried this religiously for a while and all the resulting litters still came at night!

Actual labour is clearly evident when the bitch constantly looks towards her rear end and when her abdominal contractions begin. These are absolutely unmistakable and can most accurately be described as a spasm rippling down the bitch's body from front to back and accompanied by evident pushing. The water bag is the first thing to arrive, and this usually comes along about half an hour after the first contractions. The first puppy should then follow within the next two hours. I have to say that we do not sit with our bitches continuously during this time, as it often seems as though they are waiting for you to have the puppies on their behalf. A very close and regular watch is what is required.

If the bitch goes longer than two hours, please call the vet, but hopefully this will not be necessary and a puppy will soon emerge in its bag. Following each pup or along with each pup, there will also be an afterbirth and the puppy may still have this attached to its umbilical cord. What now?

Boxers, even if they have not had a litter before, tend to make excellent, instinctive mothers and, when presented with a puppy in a bag and an afterbirth, you will invariably find that the mother breaks the bag and licks the puppy to get it going, severs the umbilical cord cleanly and eats the afterbirth – a fine source of nourishment for her. She will do all of this as if it is the most natural thing in the world, which, of course, it is.

In the unlikely event that instinct does not take over, you will need to give a hand. Your priority is to get the bag open and the

The water bag is the first thing to emerge.

The bitch will sometimes stand up during the delivery. Each puppy should emerge in a bag.

puppy breathing. You will find the bag reasonably tough and you may need your scissors. Once the puppy is out, clear the mucus away from his mouth and nose and hold his head downwards so that any fluid can drain out. By this stage, the little chap should have given a small cry and you should dry the whelp briskly with a towel.

You should do all of this in view of the bitch so that she can see what is happening and you will often find that nature clicks in halfway through and your help is no longer required. Throughout this exercise, please do be careful if the umbilical cord is still attached, as any strain on this can result in

an umbilical hernia. If the bitch does not sever the cord, encourage the fluid inside back towards the puppy and pinch it firmly about two inches away from the puppy's body. On the side of your grip which is furthest from the pup, sever the cord with your nails or the scissors. After you have made the cut, keep a firm grip for a few seconds to prevent bleeding. There is no need to knot it or tie cord around it, and it will eventually dry and drop off. You should make a note of the time that the first puppy was born, and it is also sensible to record whether or not it was accompanied by an afterbirth.

Once the first puppy has been born successfully, the rest of the whelping should be comparatively straightforward. You may find that the first-born takes a bit of a hammering before the next puppy arrives, as the bitch will be so proud and protective of her baby that she will lick and pick it up constantly. Do not worry about this too much as it will stop when she has more than one to deal with. Once puppies have started to arrive, there should not be long gaps and anything over two hours should prompt you to get the vet. You should also seek immediate veterinary assistance if a puppy gets stuck during delivery. If the puppy is not seriously stuck, you may try easing it out manually – not straight out, but in a downward motion towards the bitch's feet and only coinciding with the bitch's own contractions. However, my feeling is that this exercise is best left to more experienced whelpers and that, if there is a puppy to be manipulated out, your vet should be the one to do it.

Throughout the whelping, it is important for you to make sure that the puppies start suckling immediately. During the birth, the

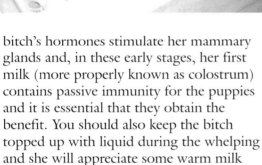

TOP LEFT: This bitch is delivering her third puppy.

ABOVE: It is very important that puppies benefit from their mother's early milk, which contains passive immunity for the litter. The puppy second from the right is just minutes old, but he is suckling already.

LEFT: Once your bitch has finished whelping, take her out to spend a penny and get a helper to quickly change all the paper and the whelping blanket. You should then let your bitch settle down quietly with her new family.

bitch's hormones stimulate her mammary glands and, in these early stages, her first milk (more properly known as colostrum) contains passive immunity for the puppies and it is essential that they obtain the benefit. You should also keep the bitch topped up with liquid during the whelping and she will appreciate some warm milk with glucose during the natural breaks.

When you eventually believe that she has finished, you must get her out of the box and make her spend a penny. While you are doing this, get a helper to nip in and change the bedding. Whelping is a very messy business and you will need to replace all the newspaper and put in a fresh Vetbed. If you have taken the bitch outside in the dark to perform her toilet, it is a sensible precaution to take a torch to make absolutely certain that she does not pass a

final puppy at the same time – it has been known!

It will have been a long night for the bitch and for you, but whelping is an experience that many breeders still enjoy enormously and, thankfully for them, the next few weeks are normally quite easy.

POSSIBLE COMPLICATIONS

What I have described above is a normal course of events and, nine times out of ten, this is how your litters will be born. However, there are occasions when things do not go quite according to plan. I stress the two-hour timeframe, because this length of delay or 'inertia' usually means that something is going wrong. Inertia can take place for a number of different reasons: malpresentation of a pup or puppies; presentation of an oversized pup; blockage of the canal by afterbirths; or just plain exhaustion. If your vet suspects this he may ask you to bring the bitch into the surgery. This is not laziness on his part. In the back of his mind will be the hope that moving the bitch to the car, and the journey, will jog things along. It often does, so make sure that you take your cardboard box, hot-water bottle and towels with you just in case. We have had quite a number of puppies born in the car either on the way to or on the way back from the vet.

If you still have no joy, the vet will most likely give your bitch a jab of pituitrin to try and get things moving. If this has no effect, he will probably repeat the injection after half an hour or so. If two injections do not result in a puppy being delivered, then your bitch will almost certainly need a Caesarean. None of us likes having puppies delivered in this way, but it is unfair on the bitch to delay any further. On the subject of Caesareans, please do make sure that your vet uses only a gaseous anaesthetic applied by a mask. This ensures that the puppies will be born full of life and will not be anaesthetised and sedated. You will also find that the bitch will recover much quicker. As these events usually take place out of hours, it is quite normal for you to be there while the Caesarean is taking place, rubbing the puppies down and getting them going while the vet concentrates on the bitch. Once again, your cardboard box and hot-water bottle will come into their own. When you get the mother and puppies home, put the puppies in the whelping box and introduce the dam as soon as she is steady on her feet. It is important that puppies born by Caesarean also benefit from the bitch's early milk.

Another problem you will sometimes be faced with is the puppy that is born apparently dead, but looking totally normal. The very definite message here is: do not give up too easily. There is a variety of techniques that you can use to revive the pup, since all you are trying to do is make it gasp and start breathing. Very rough and continued rubbing and shaking with a warm towel is often sufficient. Other breeders have had success by running the puppy first under warm water and then under a cold tap, the shock often proving sufficient to bring it round. Breathing into its mouth may also be enough or placing a drop of whisky on its tongue. All of these methods have worked, though we principally use the towel method. The trick is not to be too gentle and to keep at it – it can take anything up to twenty minutes – and you must not stop when you hear the first gasp. Keep going until the breathing has stabilised into a regular pattern. Some of these methods may sound quite harsh, but you have nothing to lose and everything to gain. After all, when you first pick it up all you have is a dead puppy and it cannot get much worse than that!

As far as the bitch is concerned, although the condition is not often seen, you must watch out for signs of possible eclampsia which can occur at any time after the birth of the puppies. This condition makes the bitch go rather wild and she will seem to stare right through you, look fixedly at her puppies and gaze into space. These symptoms will be accompanied by extreme restlessness, when the bitch is in danger of doing herself and her puppies serious injury, and she will whimper pitifully and shiver. As you can imagine, eclampsia is extremely serious and may result in collapse and death, but the cure is almost magical in its speed. The condition is caused by a calcium imbalance (which can occur even if you have been giving supplements carefully) and a jab from the vet will quickly correct matters. What is important is that you recognise the symptoms swiftly and get this treatment administered immediately.

A HELPING HAND

If your bitch has a large litter (anything over seven is large) it is often sensible to supplement the puppies. This should also be done if the bitch does not have much milk (though this would be most unusual for a Boxer), and you must be prepared to assist the mother if ever one or more of the puppies does not appear to be thriving.

Bitch's milk is significantly different to cow's milk, in that it is very rich and creamy and does not contain lactose. Puppies cannot digest lactose as they do not have the lactase enzyme to break it down, so, if pups do need supplements, a balanced milk must be given. There are many excellent substitutes for bitch's milk on the market and these may be obtained through your vet. They should be fed using a premature baby's feeding bottle. Some take to it easily, some less so, but persevere and, if possible, make sure it is always the same person who does the supplementing, as baby puppies undoubtedly do get used to one person's touch.

A VETERINARY CHECK

No matter how smoothly things have gone, we always have the vet come down and check our bitches on the day after whelping. It is notoriously difficult to tell when a Boxer bitch has finished, and it is very hard to identify whether she is retaining any puppies or afterbirths. By counting the number of afterbirths that came out with the puppies you will have one checking mechanism, but a professional examination is a good investment. To be on the safe side, your vet will probably give the bitch an antibiotic and a 'clear out' jab to make sure that she passes anything that is left inside. On this visit, we also ask the vet to give the pups a quick once-over and he will check for any abnormalities.

WHITE PUPPIES

This is a difficult subject. In any litter between flashily marked parents there is likely to be at least one white puppy. Over the years, we have seen a greater preponderance of them coming back on Boxer Rescue and they appear to have a greater propensity to deafness. For these two reasons, some breeders will not keep white puppies and they have them put to sleep at birth. On the other hand, as far as we are concerned, we have only ever had one white puppy grow up deaf and we often have homes waiting where people have had a white Boxer from us before. In these circumstances, we find it hard to justify putting a healthy puppy to sleep.

There are valid arguments for and against, and opinion is fairly evenly divided on the subject. As a breeder, it is for you to make up your own mind. However, if you are intent on culling your whites, the one thing you must do is get your vet to do this in a humane manner. Every so often you hear of people using 'do-it-yourself' techniques. This appals me.

TEMPERATURE

Throughout whelping and rearing it is essential that the correct temperature is maintained. There is no doubt that insufficient heat can be a major problem to young puppies, because they are incapable of generating heat by shivering, they have little fat to provide insulation and they have low glycogen energy reserves. If their temperature is allowed to drop, you will very soon have a disaster on your hands. A lot of warmth for the puppies will be generated by the presence of their mother in the enclosed whelping box but, as a guide, the following temperatures should be maintained in their immediate environment:

Age of puppy (weeks)	Advised temperature
0-1	29C (84F)
2-4	27C (81F)
4-6	25C (77F)
6+	21C (70F)

If you have things too cold, the puppies will be huddled together and, if you have the box too hot, they will struggle away from each other and lie on their own. In both cases they will usually be noisy and clearly distressed. A heat lamp over the whelping box is the ideal source of heat, because both the bitch and the puppies can move away from or towards the main focus of warmth as they wish.

DOCKING AND DEWCLAWS
These two simple procedures should be carried out by a vet when the puppies are about three days old, but do leave it a little longer if the puppies have been born early. As part of your preparations, you will remember that you have already identified a vet who is willing to dock the puppies. It is essential that this is planned well in advance.

Common sense tells you that you should remove the bitch from the room when the vet is attending to the puppies, and please do not allow the vet to dock the puppies' tails too short, as there is no quicker way to ruin a good dog. It is not difficult to get the length right – we look at the puppy overall and get the vet to dock its tail at a length which looks in the correct proportion for the puppy now. A more technical method is to hold the tail between the puppy's legs and dock it at the point where it passes the bottom end of the pup's anus. The width of a female index finger is also quite a good guide.

Dewclaws must be removed, and Boxers are much better off without them as adult dogs can easily catch them and do themselves an injury. It is very unusual to find them on the back feet as well, but get your vet to check.

Docking is currently a very emotive subject, but it remains legal as long as it is carried out by a vet. Our own experience is that the puppies barely make a sound when it is being done and, within minutes, they are back with the bitch and feeding contentedly.

THE NEXT THREE WEEKS
The three weeks following the birth should be straightforward times for the breeder. The dam will attend to the puppies, feeding them and keeping them clean, and your tasks are really quite simple: you must change the Vetbed twice a day; any visitors and other animals must be kept away from the litter; the dam and her puppies will appreciate peace and quiet; and you must also keep the mother very well fed. In the

At about 10 days, the puppies' eyes will begin to open.

days after whelping, feed her little, often and according to demand. When she is nursing puppies, she will need plenty of good-quality food and significantly more than normal – at least twice as much. It is almost impossible to overfeed her at this stage. However, the most important part of your job in these early days is to observe progress very closely and watch out for anything even slightly unusual.

As far as the puppies go, they should feel robust, solid and warm. They should feed eagerly and grow quickly. We do not bother weighing our puppies, but we do keep an eagle eye on them for any sign of limpness, lack of vigour, constant isolation or noisiness. Drowsy gurgles, grunts and squeaks are what you ought to hear from the whelping box. Any other noises are a sure sign that something is up. I have often heard the sound of an ailing puppy described as "like a sea-gull's call", and this is a very apt description. The noise goes right through you.

At first signs of distress, make absolutely sure that the puppy is fully warm (warmth can be a great healer) and see that he is feeding properly off the bitch. You should also start supplementing him to make sure that he is getting enough nourishment. If all of this seems to have no effect in the very short term, call the vet, as you may have a 'fading puppy' on your hands. The vet may be able to help but, if the bitch wants nothing to do with the puppy and it continues to ail despite your best endeavours, then you have a real problem. Maternal intuition is often very accurate and, sad to say, a fading puppy that is shunned by its mother will usually not survive. This is nature's way and, without wishing to sound heartless, you should not grieve too long – the death of a baby puppy is infinitely better than 'successfully' rearing a sickly adult. If you are going to lose a puppy, it normally happens in the first week.

Your regular watch on puppies should also include the area around their navels to make sure that there is no infection, and you should keep an eye open for signs of diarrhoea. Puppy motions are not firm but neither should they be liquid. An antibiotic from the vet should clear things up and a small quantity of natural yoghurt placed on the tongue works wonders.

You must also keep a close check on the dam. The best sign is for your dam to lie happily with her puppies, stretched out and allowing them to feed. If you have a dam who sits up, looks uncomfortable or pants excessively, something is not right. After whelping, it is normal for her to have a discharge from her vulva, initially dark in colour but soon lightening to normal blood-red. This can go on for a number of weeks and it is quite normal. However, if this discharge ever goes dark in colour again or starts to smell you must get the vet immediately, as these symptoms indicate an infection in the uterus or metritis (an inflammation of the uterus, possibly caused by a retained afterbirth).

By the time the litter is two and a half weeks old, you will have started weaning the puppies on to solid foods.

Mastitis is another concern. This is a condition in which the milk in one or more quarters builds up behind the nipple and may become infected. You should check your bitch's teats twice a day for any 'hot spots', swelling or lumpiness. These are sure signs of mastitis. You can ease matters by drawing off the milk manually three or four times a day from the affected teat but, if infection has set in and the milk you draw is clearly 'off', your vet will need to be involved quickly. However, prevention is the best cure and you can limit your bitch's chances of mastitis by religious cleanliness of the Vetbed and by making sure that the puppies are feeding off all nipples. Hopefully you will encounter none of these problems, but you will notice that the consistent message is one of common sense, keen observation and swift involvement of your vet.

Puppies are the greatest time-wasters in the world, and few things are more pleasurable than sitting quietly in the whelping room watching a healthy litter and contented dam. At around 10 days or so you will see that the puppies' eyes are starting to open and at this stage they will not appreciate bright light. When the eyes are fully open you will see that they are almost navy blue in colour. This is quite normal, and these eyes will end up dark in the end. It is the watery blue/green eye which will probably end up unacceptably light in later life. You will also be able to check immediately whether the third eyelids are pigmented. If they are, there will be a black rim around the membrane at the corner of the eye nearest the nose. In reality, these last two points are only considerations in a show dog.

Towards the end of this first three weeks, it is sensible to register your litter with the Kennel Club so that you have the paperwork back in good time for the sale. Most of us do not like registering puppies any earlier than this for fear that we are counting our chickens before they are properly hatched! Now is also a good time to make arrangements to have the puppies insured at point of sale.

WEANING AND FEEDING
At about two and a half weeks when they are getting up on their feet, we begin to think about starting the puppies on solids and, from this moment on, the litter should become much harder work for you and

You should make sure that your whelping room has a place where your bitch can get away from her puppies. In this instance, the mother can retreat to a shelf above the whelping box.

much less work for the dam. Getting puppies to start on solids is a very messy business indeed, as they always seem much keener to trample through their food rather than eat it.

I know that the popular method is to start puppies off on some relatively innocuous milk-based product, but we have never had much success with this as it does not seem to have much instant appeal to the babies. For our puppies we mince cooked tripe very, very finely and put it on a flat dish in the centre of the whelping box. We put the puppies around it and rub some of the food on their faces, which they promptly lick off. This is often enough to encourage them to try taking a mouthful for themselves. Maybe not all of the puppies will cotton on at the first attempt, and do not despair if some are slower than others. To improve our chances, we take the bitch out for an hour or so beforehand so that the pups are not totally stuffed with mother's goodness when we are trying to tempt them.

For the first couple of days, we try the pups once a day. They will take more each time and you should ensure that each puppy has a go – if you are not careful, the stronger ones can push the others out of the way. Once you have completed these early feedings, let the dam in afterwards to polish off any leftovers. You should gradually increase the number of meals given over the course of week three and increase the variety, until the puppies are on the following programme of four meals a day:

Breakfast: a milk-based meal such as rice pudding, scrambled egg or cereal.
Mid-morning: finely-minced meat and a small quantity of puppy meal, soaked beforehand in hot water.
Afternoon: a repeat of the mid-morning meal.
Supper: a repeat of the breakfast meal.

We feed our litters from one bowl since competition seems to sharpen the appetite, but you must continue keeping an eye on any slower 'doers' and make sure that they are not left out. Puppy feeding troughs are excellent, as these stop the puppies from clambering through their food and they ensure that every pup gets a fair crack at it. As soon as you have started feeding your puppies, you will find that they progress rapidly both mentally and physically. The whelping box should be opened up and they should be allowed to explore their surroundings. You will also find that once they start feeding, the dam quickly stops cleaning up after them and this becomes another job for you.

During the weaning process, the litter are obviously becoming less dependent on their mother and, within the whelping room, the bitch should have a space where she is able to escape from her puppies. You should start to formally separate her from them for part of the day when they start to feed properly and, by the time they are on four meals daily, she should be separated from them all day, though she must be returned to sleep with them until they have turned six weeks. You should have no problems with this increasing separation and, although she will be happy to go back in with her pups after a period away, she should not be frantic to reach them. After six weeks, the puppies will be fully weaned and the bitch can just be put in very occasionally for short periods to help drain her off.

EAR CROPPING

In many parts of the world, including the UK, the cropping of ears is banned. I must say that I am not unhappy about this, for although there is no doubt in my mind that a Boxer looks magnificent with cropped ears, this practice does entail a general anaesthetic on your young puppies.

Where it is permitted, most breeders have the whole litter cropped when the pups are between seven and nine weeks old, because doing it early seems to improve the ears' chances of standing up well. The most important consideration of all is to use a vet who is proficient at cropping. Make no mistake, this is quite an art form and it needs to be done well.

Once the operation has been carried out, the ears need to be allowed to heal for a few days before they can be positioned and, during this time, you will need to treat the edges with an antiseptic powder. It is only after the stitches have been removed that you can really start the exercise of getting the ears to stand up. There are many different ways of achieving this, some using the traditional method of taping, while others use a technique which involves foam. However, because you only have one chance to get it right, this is a job for the experts, so follow the advice of the breeder or your vet precisely and, with luck, you will end up with a perfectly erect set of ears. You can play your part in helping to achieve this by giving regular Vitamin C supplements to help in the formation of good connective tissue.

In countries where it is legal, ear cropping is generally carried out at 7-9 weeks of age. This is the famous American Champion, Kiebla's Tradition of TuRo and her son, whose ears were cropped a few weeks earlier and are now 'posted' into position.
Photo: Marcia.

EARLY HEALTH CARE

Worming is a most essential exercise. Some vets now recommend worming the bitch in the early stages of her pregnancy in the belief that this will reduce the puppies' worm burden, but, in any event, you will need to worm the pups when they are three weeks old. Your vet will be able to supply you with one of the many excellent and easily administered preparations on the market. The puppies will then need worming again after another three weeks.

You must also take care of the puppies' nails. These should be kept trimmed every week from a week old, to make sure of neat nails in the adult and to stop the puppies scratching the bitch uncomfortably when they feed.

The other important part of 'health care' is to make sure that you spend enough time handling and socialising your pups. A radio playing in the whelping room can be helpful in getting them used to noise and you should supply a lot of simple (and cheap!) toys. Old slippers, a pair of old socks knotted together, empty cartons and the like will all provide endless amusement.

PROSPECTIVE PURCHASERS

Much as you will have enjoyed your litter, by the time you have them fully weaned you will be realising what a handful puppies can be and how much attention and food they need. Your thoughts will quickly turn to prospective purchasers!

Sometimes, you will find that the owner of the stud dog you used gets more puppy enquiries than he can fulfil, and he may be willing to pass one or two your way. You may also contact the secretary of the local breed club to which you belong, in case any possible sales are routed that way. In some countries, it is also possible to pay a fee direct to the national Kennel Club when you register a litter and, in return, they will send any potential purchasers who contact them direct to you.

So, there are a number of ways that you can find potential buyers but, as you can see, a lot of these do rely on other people. Consequently, it is always sensible to place an advert in one of your local papers as a back-stop. The one thing you can be absolutely sure of is that everyone else in the Boxer world will seem to have litters to sell at exactly the same time as you!

THE SALE

As a responsible breeder, you will want to make certain that your puppies go into good homes so, when potential buyers come to see the litter, please make sure that the whole family come along. It is important for you to see that all members of the family want the dog. Personally, I think that you can learn a lot from watching how potential buyers react to your other dogs and by having an open conversation with them when they are looking at the litter and ascertaining: whether they have had a dog before; what their working arrangements are; whether they have considered all the drawbacks; what they want the dog for; whether they have done their research properly; do they have a garden?; is it properly fenced?; do they have any other animals?; do their children burst into tears when confronted by one of your adult dogs?; does the family mind when one of the dogs jumps up to greet them and puts dirty great paw-marks all down their clothes?

You can very quickly begin to build up a mental profile which will help you to decide

Although Boxer puppies are very appealing, you will be glad to find them good homes when they are eight weeks old!

whether the people in front of you would make suitable owners for one of your puppies. We breeders have all been fooled, however; some people have read all the books and spin a good yarn when they come along, only to turn into poor long-term owners. Then there are the ones you agonise over who actually give their puppy a super home. We cannot be right all of the time and, in an ideal world, it would be nice to sell Boxers only to people who have owned the breed before and have just lost an oldie, but this is not always possible – we all had to start somewhere. Within reason, we tend to give people the benefit of the doubt.

When you are trying to sell your pups, it is sensible to establish beforehand (maybe from the stud dog owner) what is a reasonable price to charge, and you should take a deposit from your buyers when they have committed themselves. At the time of purchase, you should give the new owners the registration certificate, a pedigree, a sales receipt, an insurance certificate covering the next six weeks of the puppy's life, and a full feeding chart.

THE AFTER-SALES SERVICE
At the time of sale you should assure the purchaser that, if they have any problems with the puppy at any time during its life, they should feel free to speak to you immediately. In the unlikely event that they become unable to cope with the dog and need to rehome it, they must promise to get in contact with you first for assistance. This is all part of responsible dog-breeding and you do not want a reputation for clogging up the rescue services with dogs that you bred and homed carelessly.

THE BITCH
A good dam is worth her weight in gold and she will put everything she has into her puppies. Despite your very best endeavours with excellent feeding and care, this will sometimes mean that she emerges from the other side of motherhood looking a bit moth-eaten. In particular, it is common for bitches to lose a lot of their coat and some find it hard to keep weight on while feeding pups.

After they have finished with their brood, we tend to strip through the loose coat lightly and give the bitches a good bath to freshen them up. Most importantly, we continue feeding them very well and we exercise them regularly. If they are particularly droopy underneath a frequent rub-down with some camphorated oil or (in good weather) an occasional light hosing with cold water will help. Once she is fully off her puppies, you will be amazed at how quickly your dam returns to her original condition. Indeed, some mothers look even better for having had a litter.

11 THE MODERN BRITISH BOXER

In the post-war years, the popularity of the Boxer has grown steadily. For some time, in terms of numbers registered annually by the Kennel Club, the breed has been among the country's top ten – a fact also reflected in show ring numbers, where the Boxer entry is often the largest in the Working Group. During its development in the UK, the breed has been well served by a large number of keen enthusiasts who have worked hard to bring Boxers up to their current high standard. Many of the breeders who achieved so much in the early years are no longer with us or they have now largely retired from active breeding and showing; some very famous kennel names fall into this category and they are mentioned in Chapter One. However, in this chapter, we bring things right up to date by looking at the achievements of Boxer breeders who continue to improve the breed today.

To mention everyone would clearly be impossible so, for my review of the modern UK Boxer scene, I have had to limit myself to those kennels which have owned or bred three or more UK Champions and who are still winning at the highest level in the 1990s show ring. You will notice that the list includes many long-standing breeders who continue to turn out top-quality stock, but there are also some newer names who have achieved considerable success in recent years. This is the strength of our breed. It is no closed shop dominated by names from history. It is a broad spectrum of exhibitors, from all walks of life and from all ages, just doing their best to improve the overall quality of UK Boxers.

BUCKSTEPS
Jenny and Peter Whittaker

For many years this kennel has had a strong reputation for consistently producing typical Boxers with excellent heads and expressions. After several CC and Reserve CC winners, they bred their first Champion in the early 1980s. This was the brindle bitch Ch. Bucksteps Bit o' Bother at Jenroy, who was sold to Jenny Townshend as a puppy. A few years later, they had more success with Ch. Bucksteps Honeymoon, who won very well throughout her career and ended up with 5 CCs. Moving into the 90s, the Whittakers had mated one of their Famous Grouse daughters to the Broughtons' Ch. Glenfall The Gladiator,

Ch. Bucksteps Bittersweet, Boxer of the Year 1997.

at the National finals held in Cheltenham and then, a few months later, Charlie Brown went Best of Breed at Crufts under Philip Greenway and his sister won the Reserve Bitch CC. It does not come much better than that!

CARINYA
Daphne North
Based just north of Chepstow, Daphne North quietly breeds her Boxers. The Carinya line is based heavily on Marian Fairbrother's famous Gremlin breeding, which was well known to Daphne since she used to handle the Gremlin dogs during Marian's final years, making up her last Champion. In the late 1970s, Daphne bred a daughter of US import Kreyons Back in Town of Winuwuk to the one-time breed record holder Ch. Gremlin Summer Storm. This mating resulted in Ch. Carinya Petticoat, a really well-made brindle bitch with a lovely balanced outline. A few years on, Daphne used the Summer Storm son Glenmorangie a couple of times, and she made up a daughter of his, Ch. Carinya Candle in the Wind. She also had a very promising dog puppy of similar breeding called Cnochon Wood whom I remember judging as a youngster and making Best Puppy. He was destined for great things, but, sadly, Daphne lost him soon after. Glenmorangie was also the sire of the biggest-winning Carinya to date, Ch. Carinya Rye 'n' Dry who was born in March 1988 out of one of the last Gremlin bitches, Change Key. Bred by Daphne, he was given to Debbie Theaker who campaigned him. The famous German judge Karin Rezewski awarded him his first CC just out of puppy at the Northern Boxer Club, and he went on to win 23 CCs

and one of the resulting bitch puppies was going to prove a real asset to the kennel. 'Floozie' (more formally known as Bucksteps Easy Virtue) was not shown, but she has proved to be a very good brood bitch. Mated twice to Ch. Carinya Rye 'n' Dry, she produced Ch. Bucksteps Charlie Brown and then Ch. Bucksteps Bittersweet. Floozie's influence has also continued into the next generation because another of her daughters by Rye 'n' Dry was mated back to The Gladiator to produce Ch. Bucksteps Chariots of Fire at Dallgerry, who was sold as a puppy to Ann Podmore. Bittersweet and Charlie Brown won their Champion titles swiftly and they also gave Jenny and Peter a wonderful start to 1997. In January, Bittersweet was crowned Boxer of the Year in all. We do not see Daphne at all the shows, but, when she does attend, she is one of those who remains fascinated with judging, watching intently all day. She is currently campaigning Cheers for Carinya, who was Best Puppy in Show at the British Boxer Club a few years back and who has recently won his first CC.

FAERDORN
Sue Harvey

Sue Harvey's father was a butcher, and one of his customers had three Boxers. It was here that Sue's interest in the breed began, and she quickly progressed from schoolgirl to one of the most talented dog breeders in the game. Her early lines were based on the great American import Rainey-Lane's Sirrocco and the first Faerdorn Champion was a Sirrocco grand-daughter. This was Ch. Faerdorn Truly Scrumptious, who started her show career in sensational style by winning her first CC and the Group aged just nine months, at the Hove Championship Show in 1969, starting the family tradition of Boxers capable of winning well in all-breed competition. After taking her title, she was mated to Int. Ch. Seefeld Picasso and Sue campaigned one of her daughters, Truly Gorgeous, to her title in partnership with the Somerfields. Since those early days, there have been many exceptional Faerdorns, including the biggest winner, Ch. Faerdorn Pheasant Plucker, who won 24 CCs, five Groups and a Best in Show All-Breeds under Bill Taylor at the SKC. Pheasant Plucker was in the ring at the same time as Ch. Norwatch Brock Buster and Open Dog was keenly contested – we can only guess at how many tickets these two would have won if they had been born a few more years apart.

Ch. Faerdorn Fineas Fogg, a recent winner of the British Boxer Club's Sire of Merit award.
Photo: Banks.

Sue Harvey is one of those true dog breeders, whose motivation lies more in the whelping box than in the show ring, and, because of this, she has been happy to sell winners to other exhibitors over the years. No breeder has a greater reputation for doing this than Sue: Ch. Faerdorn Head Over Heels to Santonoaks was campaigned to Group success by Vince and Annabel Zammit; Ch. Faerdorn Whatever Next at Sulez and Ch. Faerdorn So Glad for Sulez have been made up by Sue Drinkwater; Ch. Faerdorn With Love to Shiloh won her title (and a Crufts Best of Breed!) for Stuart Lockwood-Brown and Tony Curtin; Ch. Faerdorn Flash Bang Wallop was made up for Carol Evans; and Ch. Faerdorn Easy Lover at Lacreme was campaigned by Joe Chadwick. These have all been in addition to the Champions kept at home, like Knobs 'n' Knockers and most recently Fineas Fogg, the current British Boxer Club Sire of Merit, who is quickly making a name for himself as a stud force.

GLENFALL
Pam and Ken Broughton
Based at their lovely home in the

Ch. Glenfall Clever Clogs, the lovely headed daughter of Dutch Import Anja von Dommeldal of Glenfall.

acquisition to strengthen the kennel's bitch line was the Dutch import Anja von Dommeldal of Glenfall. When mated to The Gladiator, she produced the aptly named Ch. Glenfall Wicked Wanda and then, to Famous Grouse, she produced the beautifully headed Ch. Glenfall Clever Clogs and the Reserve CC-winning Glenfall Hit the Heights of Tynteville. Anja was awarded the Dam of Merit trophy by the British Boxer Club in 1990 and, through her children, she is also behind Ch. Fletcher at Sunhawk Norwatch and Ch. Tyegarth Pacherenc at Seacrest. Anja has turned out to be a most influential Boxer. The Broughtons also campaigned Ch. Tyegarth Jurancon of Glenfall to his title and they have some lovely winning youngsters in the ring at present.

JENROY
Jenny and Roy Townshend
As they lived quite close to Sheila Cartwright at the time, the Townshends had gone to see the repeat mating of Famous Grouse in the nest and they ended up buying a promising dog puppy. He soon became Ch. Tyegarth Glenmorangie of Jenroy, the Townshends' first Champion, who won the CC and Best of Breed at Crufts in 1980 when he was just over a year old. Like his brother, Glenmorangie was an excellent stud dog and his daughter, Ch. Bucksteps Bit o' Bother at Jenroy, was made up by Jenny in 1985. Bit o' Bother was subsequently mated to Ch. Norwatch Brock Buster and this resulted in Ch. Jenroy Lot Less Bother who was a truly stunning Boxer bitch – I remember loving her throughout her career. Through her children, Lot Less Bother has had a very important impact upon the British Boxer,

Cotswolds, Pam and Ken Broughton have bred Boxers on a small scale for many years, with all their dogs spending some time in the house. Although they purposely do not keep large numbers, the Broughtons have enjoyed much success in the ring and, almost uniquely, they have combined English, American and Continental lines into their family of good-looking Boxers. I always think that the Glenfalls are characterised by outstanding expressions and lovely eyes – their particular favourite, Winuwuk Back in Fashion of Glenfall, certainly had these attributes.

The first Glenfall Champion, The Gladiator, was born in the mid-1980s and he has subsequently proved to be a useful stud dog. He was the British Boxer Club Sire of Merit in 1995, and his direct influence is still there to this day with another two sons and a daughter becoming Champions in 1997. An important

Ch. Jenroy Lot Less Bother was a good producer and her breeding is very close up in the pedigrees of several top winners.

since her daughter (Jenroy Popsicle for Belmont) produced the brindle record holder, Ch. Roamaro Scotch Mist of Winuwuk, and her son (Jenroy Pop Back to Walkon) produced the 1995 and 1996 Top Boxer in the UK, Ch. Blueprint Beern Skittles at Walkon, along with many big winners in his native Australia. The latest Jenroy Champion, Edge of Darkness, is also a Lot Less Bother son.

In the mid-80s, by doing a father-to-daughter mating on Glenmorangie, the Townshends produced their biggest winner, Ch. Jenroy Pop My Cork to Walkon, whom they sold to the Millers as a baby. Pop My Cork won 21 CCs and he was also a Working Group winner. Jenny loved watching him win, and her finest hour came when Pop My Cork was Boxer of the Year at the National finals and her own Lot Less Bother was Best Opposite Sex.

As well as winners for the home kennel,

Glenmorangie sired many more Champions for other breeders and his stock won over 50 CCs in the UK alone.

MANIC
Julie Cook

At the Bath Championship Show in 1989, Julie won her first CC with the elegant bitch, Manic Won't It. Not long after, she managed to persuade Vince and Annabel Zammit to let her have a lovely dark brindle and white bitch puppy who had already started a good show career. Ch. Santonoaks Kiwi Magic of Manic quickly gained her title in Julie's hands, ending up with a nice number of CCs. As her name suggests, she was sired by Ch. Tyegarth Blue Kiwi.

During Kiwi Magic's campaign, Julie purchased a dog puppy from Sue Drinkwater out of the outstanding brood bitch, Ch. Faerdorn Whatever Next at Sulez. This golden brindle boy, Ch. Sulez Whatever You Want for Manic, became a Champion but, unusually, he was beaten to it by his pretentious young daughter, Ch. Time to Dance at Manic, who was made up a few months before. Time to Dance had been bred by Jean Harding and was bought in by Julie. Among her many top awards, she was both Boxer of the Year and Best of Breed at Crufts in 1995. I was often up

Ch. Time to Dance at Manic, Boxer of the Year 1995 and Best of Breed at Crufts in the same year.

against her with Scotch Mist and I considered her strong competition – she was an excellent Boxer bitch with personality plus. I was very sorry when I heard that Julie had lost her shortly after she had whelped her first litter.

MARBELTON
Mary and John Hambleton
Over 20 English Champions have carried the Marbelton affix and their Boxers have won over 175 CCs, which is an outstanding record. Ch. Marbelton Desperate Dan was a very big winner for the kennel in the 1970s and, at one time, he was the breed record holder with 29 CCs. He also went Best of Breed at Crufts on three occasions. Moving into the 80s, the Hambletons started to bring in imports from Continental Europe with good success. The red male from Germany, Dandy von Starenschloss, produced lovely heads and eyes and he sired a couple of Champion bitches for the kennel.

Dandy also sired a bitch called Marbelton Sugar Cube, who was eventually mated to their glamorous Dutch import Quinto Manolito van der Klappeheide. This mating resulted in 'Floyd', also known as Ch. Marbelton Dressed to Kill, who was unbeaten in his puppy classes and went on to win 26 CCs along with much acclaim in the Group and Best in Show rings. I well remember following his career avidly, and I particularly recall watching him take the Group and Reserve Best in Show at the West of England Ladies' Kennel Society under Bobby James, a week before he took the top spot at Birmingham National under Bob Russell-Roberts. He had many other Group, Best and Reserve Best in Show awards and, in 1985, he was the Top

Ch. Marbelton Dressed to Kill, one of the most successful Boxers ever in all-breed competition and a great showman.

Ch. Look No Further at Marbelton, a beautiful bitch with a super outline.

Working Dog and number three all-breeds, only beaten by the Crufts Best in Show winning Standard Poodle and Airedale. It was always a pleasure to see Floyd in the ring.

John and Mary are hospitable folk and I remember accompanying Mary Foan to their kennels on one occasion. This was the era of Dandy, Quinto and Floyd, Ch.

Wanderobo Hurley Burley of Marbelton, Ch. Moljon Dream Again of Marbelton, Ch. Marbelton Drunken Duncan and many more besides. Visiting that day was like taking a trip into the Who's Who of Boxers. It was also the first time that I had seen their latest Dutch import, Dolf the Buhe Farm of Marbelton, who was destined to become one of the most successful imported sires of all time. He was possibly the most instantly appealing Boxer I have ever seen, with his copybook personality reflecting through those lovely eyes.

A few years later, the Hambletons imported Abgar von Bernamariek of Marbelton who was another stunning dog from the Continent. He made a tremendous impression on UK exhibitors when he was featured on the front cover of *Boxer Quarterly* at its launch at the British Boxer Club Golden Jubilee Championship Show, and this impression was confirmed when you met Abgar in real life.

Dolf is solidly behind the Hambletons' biggest bitch winner, Ch. Look No Further at Marbelton, who won 12 CCs and was Boxer of the Year in 1989, following on from Drunken Duncan who had won the same award a few years previously. I always remember Look No Further's very well-balanced and unexaggerated outline. The Hambletons continue to do very well with their Boxers and they are very talented dog breeders, confirmed by the fact that, within a very short space of time, they have also started winning CCs with homebred Pugs.

MINDENWOOD
Shirley and Arthur Butters
Shirley and Arthur Butters bought their first Boxer in 1952 and she produced their first real show dog, The Mindenwood Masterpiece, who was sired by Allon Dawson's well-regarded import, Frolich von Dom. After a few years of steady success, the Butters bought from Audrey Stephenson a promising brindle and white dog puppy, who was sired by Top Mark, one of the early Marbelton Champions. This puppy made up into Ch. Seacrest Drummage of Mindenwood who gained his title with a few tickets to spare. In time, one of Drummage's daughters was mated to Ch. Newlaithe Quibbler and this produced Ch. Mindenwood Jake the Fake, a dog with a lovely head and expression whom Shirley made up in 1982. Into the 90s, the Butters were fortunate to share in the many successes of Ch. Carinya Rye 'n' Dry, who was owned by their daughter Debbie Theaker. Rye 'n' Dry was a very well-made Boxer and his sound movement often found favour with Group judges. In 1992, Shirley and Arthur bought in one of his puppies from Margaret McGoohan so that they could campaign her and, in 1996, Ch. Langbarn Lily Langtry of Mindenwood gained her title.

NEWLAITHE
Christine Beardsell
Patrick and Christine Beardsell established their Yorkshire-based Newlaithe kennels with the foundation bitch Maisu Teddygirl, who had been bred by Olive Ryman. After a couple of litters to different dogs, she was mated to Ch. Hazefield Barrister and produced a litter, in December 1968, which contained a glorious red and white show girl called Newlaithe Ariadne who made up very quickly. She won a total of 11 CCs, as well as the Group at Three Counties in 1971 where she was also third in line for Best in Show. Having had this early success

with the Hazefield line, Patrick and Christine bought Best Seller from Hazel Izett and eventually mated her to Rytonways Tamouray Dark Intrigue, who was closely bred to Wardrobes stock. This produced the brindle male, Ch. Newlaithe Quibbler.

Sadly, PA took its toll on some of the early Newlaithe stock and new lines had to be established. The Beardsells went to North America and brought back some quality Boxers including Ch. Jacquet's Brass Image who was one of America's big winners at the time. However, it was through incorporating some of the Walkers' Lynpine breeding in the 1980s that top show ring successes started again, when the Beardsells put the dog they had bought in, Lynpine Cannon, to their own Arko of Lynpine daughter to produce Newlaithe Marietta, who became a Champion in 1991. A few years later, the American breeding tied up with more Lynpine breeding when Newlaithe Fashion Print, a descendant of Brass Image, was mated to the Walkers' latest import, Spanish Ch. Janos de Loermo of Lynpine. This litter contained Ch. Newlaithe Hot Fashion who gained her title in 1995. Sadly, Patrick died in 1997, but Christine continues the line.

NORWATCH-SUNHAWK
Helen and Eddie Banks

The Top Boxer Dam of all time forms the cornerstone of this Lincolnshire-based kennel. Norwatch Mustang Wine did win a Reserve CC in the ring, but it is as a wonderful brood bitch that she will always be remembered, producing five UK titleholders who won nearly 60 CCs between them. Ch. Norwatch Brock Buster, sired by Ch. Steynmere Night Rider, was her most famous son, winning 29 CCs along with many successes in all-breed competition. He won all the major awards, from Champion of Champions to Best of Breed at Crufts, and he was the consummate showman, with a personality to die for. His brother, Ch. Norwatch Glory Boy of Rayfos, was campaigned by the Greenways and he subsequently proved to be a very useful stud dog for them and the breed. A third brother, Ch. Norwatch O'Toole of Rayfos, also won his title. Mustang Wine's other two Champions were the delightful Grouse sisters, Ch. Slightly Sloshed of Sunhawk at Walkon and Ch. Norwatch Slightly Sozzled. Sozzled remains one of my all-time favourites.

Not ones to rest on their laurels, Helen and Eddie have cleverly furthered this line and have continued to produce smashing Boxers of consistent type. The Buster daughter they purchased and made up, Ch. Sheffordian Ruby Tuesday of Norwatch, produced well for them, and one of her sons was Ch. Norwatch Sunhawk Raffles, who won his title with something to spare, including a Crufts CC from Joy Malcolm. In turn, Raffles was mated back to Slightly Sloshed, and this resulted in Ch. Mitchum at Sunhawk Norwatch, who subsequently went to Australia, but not before he had sired Ch. Fletcher at Sunhawk Norwatch. Fletcher was then mated back to Ruby Tuesday to produce Ch. Norwatch Sunhawk Wanneroo, who was the top Boxer male in 1993. Wanneroo then sired their Champion bitch, Scandal. When Scandal was made up, this gave the kennel a direct line of seven UK titleholders which is a unique breeding achievement.

Helen Banks is one of the very best 'hands-on' Boxer handlers in the world, and

Norwatch Mustang Wine pictured with two of her Champion children, Ch. Norwatch Brock Buster and Ch. Norwatch Slightly Sozzled.

Photo: Banks.

she has proved quite a role model for others to follow, but there is no point being an outstanding handler if you do not have the dogs to go with it. Thankfully, the Banks have always had the outstanding dogs too.

RAYFOS
Barbara and Philip Greenway
Few people have had as many good dogs through their hands as the Greenways since, as well as their own dogs, Philip has also handled many outstanding Boxers for other kennels. Ch. Rayfos Rainmaker was their own first big winner, collecting 13 tickets in the 1960s, but, after this, their own breeding activities were curtailed as Philip concentrated on the serious business of professional handling. Eventually, the Greenways resumed their own Boxer exhibiting with Ch. Norwatch Glory Boy of Rayfos whom they had bought from Helen Banks. Glory Boy then sired Barbara's pride and joy, Ch. Rayfos Cock Robin, who was out of Rayfos 'Arf a Tick, a daughter of the American Import Salgray's Minute Man. Cock Robin was in the ring at the same time as Ch. Marbelton Dressed to Kill and so competition was intense, but he picked up 26 CCs and the record as the top winning red male of all time. He was also Best in Show out of 502 at the British

Boxer Club's Golden Jubilee Championship Show in 1986. It is some record that, 10 years later, Philip was also the handler of the Diamond Jubilee Best in Show winner, Ch. Kenbru Mollyhawk.

Ch. Ice Maiden of Rayfos, Ch. Norwatch O'Toole of Rayfos, and Ch. Freedom Fighter for Rayfos have also been made up by the Greenways and, in recent years, Philip was almost invariably found on the end of the lead during the record-breaking campaign of Ch. Tonantron Glory Lass, a bitch who gave him tremendous pleasure. Recently, I had the pleasure of a long lunch with the Greenways and it is clear that they simply enjoy good dogs, no matter who owns them. They also have a breadth of outlook which comes from a close involvement with several different breeds, and their Champion Terriers are even more famous than their Boxers.

SANTONOAKS
Vince and Annabel Zammit
In the late 1980s, Santonoaks quickly became a force to be reckoned with in the Boxer ring. Their Ch. Tyegarth Blue Kiwi was a great showman and he picked up in excess of 20 CCs, as well as the Boxer of the Year title in 1990 when his Champion daughter was runner-up. Indeed, Blue Kiwi

sired several good winners for the home kennel, including the three Champions – Slick Sammy, Kiwi Magic and Moody Blue. Vince and Annabel also bred and exhibited the red male, Ch. Santonoaks Robbie Redcoat who was by Glory Boy. When his first crop of puppies hit the ring, Robbie Redcoat soon became a popular stud dog and he produced very consistently. Sue Harvey used him on Ch. Faerdorn Knobs 'n' Knockers and the Zammits bought a stunning red and white bitch from the litter called Ch. Faerdorn Head Over Heels to Santonoaks. She was a spectacular show girl and, along with her first couple of CCs, she won two Groups and a Reserve Best in Show All-Breeds. She continued to win very well in the UK until she was exported to Malta where she broke many records.

Vince and Annabel parted company soon after, but Annabel kept the Santonoaks affix going and returned to the ring with a bang in 1996, exhibiting the Robbie Redcoat grand-daughter Santonoaks Be Bop a Lula, who has just become a Champion at a young age.

SEACREST
Claire Kay
This affix was started by Audrey Stephenson but, in recent years, it has achieved very good show successes in the hands of her daughter, Claire Kay. In 1990, Claire obtained a very smart brindle bitch

from the Skelder kennel called Comedy of Errors and she campaigned her to a title which included a Crufts CC. Shortly afterwards, she obtained from Sheila Cartwright a brindle dog who also became a Champion but, more importantly, Ch. Tyegarth Pacherenc at Seacrest was to prove his worth as a stud dog, being the top sire in the breed from 1994 to 1997. Angela Harper mated her Huttonvale Highlight bitch to him on several occasions with great success and Claire bought and campaigned one of the puppies, Ch. Huttonvale High Command at Seacrest. High Command now has a large number of CCs and has been Best Dog at the Dog of the Year finals on a couple of occasions. Over the years, Claire has also bought in some bitches to strengthen her kennel further, and one of these was Porth Pearl Diver who is heavily bred on Glenfall lines. Mated to one of Paul Russell's dogs, she produced the home-bred Champion Seacrest Sassafras at Quantro, who was shown by Philip Greenway for David James. Her crowning CC, with Best in Show, came at the British Boxer Club.

Claire has won CCs or Reserves with a number of other dogs through the years and she currently has a strong team. She is a highly dedicated exhibitor who always gets the very best from her Boxers in the ring and I do not think I have ever seen a Seacrest Boxer not giving 100 per cent.

SEEFELD
Pat Heath
Based in Somerset, the Seefeld kennel is part of that elite band whose dogs have won more than 100 CCs. Pat Heath has so far bred or owned 15 English Champions,

The big winning Ch. Huttonvale High Command at Seacrest won his first CC at just 10 months of age.

and some of these have excelled in more than just the show ring. The first Seefeld Champion, Holbein, is still the only English Boxer Champion to have qualified for the prestigious C.D.(ex.) title, and this reflects Pat's keen interest in brains as well as beauty. Her best-known winner, International Ch. Seefeld Picasso, was also a true 'all-rounder'. Picasso had a super show career, and his 24 CCs in the UK made him the red male record holder for many years. He also did some useful winning in Southern Ireland where he was top dog all-breeds in 1971 and wherever he went, his outstanding show temperament and style won him many friends. On top of all his successes in the show ring, he quickly established a reputation as a dominant stud dog and, with 18 English Champions to his credit, he remains the breed's all-time top sire. Just in case he got bored, Pat worked him in the obedience ring too. Yes, Picasso was a great Boxer in any language and his influence to this day is clear.

The list of Seefeld Champions has continued uninterrupted over the years and it has been helped by the inclusion of some carefully selected imports of American breeding. One of these, Braemerwood Proclamation of Seefeld, was steeped in the famous Salgray breeding, and he was a most useful acquisition in the 1980s. Proclamation started a line of three red Champion males for the kennel, which culminated in Ch. Ashgate Able Seaman of Seefeld who won 14 CCs and was Boxer of the Year in 1993 and who is now proving to be a very dominant stud dog. I consider him to be one of the best-made Boxers that I have ever seen, with an exceptional front and forehand. I saw him only a few weeks ago and, at the age of seven, he still looks

wonderful. Like all great dogs, age has not coarsened him at all.

Pat Heath is a most knowledgeable lady on all manner of subjects, and those of us fortunate enough to have chatted at length with her feel privileged to have done so. The success of her Seefeld Boxers is testament to this knowledge and her ability to put it into practice.

SKELDER
Joy Malcolm

Finemere Betti was given to Joy Malcolm as a wedding present and all the subsequent Skelder Boxers have this bitch in their pedigree. Among them are some very well-known Champions and four who have also done the breed proud in the Group ring. The first Skelder to win a Championship Show Group was Joy's biggest winner, Ch. Skelder Burnt Almond, who won 19 CCs, and she was soon followed by her brother, Ch. Skelder Scorching. Ch. Skelder Corn Dolly then followed at Darlington in the late 1980s and, bringing things right up to the present day, Skelder Whisper Who Dares won at the major Birmingham National show in 1997.

I well remember meeting two of Joy's other Champions, Singing Sleuth and Pot Luck, on a glorious summer's day at her grand country home in Dorset. We were sitting down having tea outside the orangery and these two Boxers were brought round to parade on the large, well-manicured lawn which swept down to a brook. They looked lovely, the backdrop was perfect, and the Swedish guests I had taken were suitably impressed! Pot Luck was a top winner right from the start of her career, and her finest hour came when she won the bitch CC at the British Boxer Club

Ch. Skelder Corn Dolly is one of four Group winners campaigned by Joy Malcolm.

Golden Jubilee Show under Peggy Haslam.

Joy has proved herself to be a very clever breeder over the years, going out to use external stud dogs when she needs to, but carefully retaining the virtues of her own line when she does so. She is also an astute judge of the breed and I have noticed on several overseas trips her uncanny ability to sum up Boxers concisely and objectively at first sight.

STEYNMERE
Bruce Cattanach

Bruce Cattanach is one of the few modern Boxer exhibitors who attended the first British Boxer Club Championship Show back in 1946, but it was not until he had returned from a spell working in America that the show ring successes of the Steynmeres really began. By this time he was married to Margaret and they brought back an American bitch, Black Rose of Cherokee Oaks, who was to prove a useful foundation. When mated to Picasso, she produced Ch. Steynmere Ritzi Miss who won her first CC at just eight months and was made up at Crufts. Ritzi was the start of a direct line of six UK titleholders for Steynmere, and among these was Ch.

Steynmere Night Rider, who delighted the Cattanachs as a dominant stud dog, producing Boxers who won almost 70 CCs, including the great Ch. Norwatch Brock Buster and Ch Trywell Twelfth Night. Another of Night Rider's sons was the dramatic red male, Ch. Garnet Gelert of Steynmere, who went Best of Breed under Connie Wiley, on her last-ever judging appointment at Bournemouth in 1986, before going on to win the Group and Best in Show all breeds – a great achievement. Gelert certainly had that extrovert show personality which has characterised the Steynmeres over the years and which Bruce channels so well in the ring. I always think that Bruce is one of the most talented handlers in the ring and he makes it look so easy. Sadly, Margaret died very unexpectedly in 1996 leaving a large gap, but Bruce is still seen around the shows with top-quality stock.

SULEZ
Sue Drinkwater

When she bought Faerdorn Whatever Next from Sue Harvey, Sue Drinkwater could not have hoped for a better buy. Whatever Next became an easy Champion and, when mated to Ch. Bitza Shout and Roar, she produced Ch. Sulez Whatever You Say and Ch. Sulez Whatever You Want for Manic, as well as several CC and Reserve CC winners who have bred on. After a couple of successful litters to the same dog, Sue decide to mate Whatever Next to the Banks' young Champion, Wanneroo, for a change. In the first generation this did not appear to have worked quite as well, but one of these puppies, when mated, produced Ch. Sulez Labelled With Love, who has a fistful of CCs already and looks set to win more. I

The very successful brood bitch Ch. Faerdorn Whatever Next at Sulez....

Photo: Pearce.

...and her grand-daughter, Ch. Sulez Labelled With Love, 1997's Top Boxer.

gave her a Reserve CC as a youngster in stiff competition, rating her very highly. In the meantime, Sue had also obtained, from Sue Harvey, Faerdorn So Glad whom she christened 'Cher' because she was going to 'share' her with husband Les! Even though she was being campaigned against her other winning bitch, Sue has recently been successful in making Cher into a Champion as well.

Sue has a very nice line going, with some excellent bitches, and the way she goes about her showing and breeding has won her many friends. When I last saw her, she had another promising bitch puppy on the end of the lead winning a first prize....and so it goes on.

TIRKANE
Ann and Millicent Ingram
Considering that there are only two sets of CCs on offer in Northern Ireland each year, I hand out a special award to the Ingrams who have so far made up five Champions in the British Boxer ring during show campaigns that have involved an enormous

amount of travelling from their home just outside Belfast. Millicent's life in Boxers traces right back to the very start of the breed in the UK, and she actually won the Open Dog class at the very first British Boxer Club Championship show, judged by the famous American expert, Jack Wagner, in Coventry just after the war. Since that time, the Tirkane Boxers have established quite a reputation in the British and Irish rings and Millicent, together with her

Ch. Tirkane Auditor, made up by the Ingrams.
Photo: Pearce.

daughter Ann, are regular visitors to the mainland. Ch. Tirkane Avaunt was the top CC-winning bitch in 1975 and Champions Auditor, Chequers, Toy Boy and Teddy Boy soon followed. Toy Boy also achieved some success in the big ring, going runner-up in the Working Group at his local Belfast show after he had won his first CC and Best of Breed from Andrew Brace.

For a number of years, many of us have been treated to outstanding hospitality by the Ingrams during the annual pilgrimage to the two shows that make up the 'Irish weekend'. Lots of memories have been made sitting in the conservatory at the Cranmore Pet's Hotel.

TONANTRON
Brian and Sagra Tonkin
The Tonkins shot to fame in 1983 when their brindle and white dog, Ch. Antron Prize Guy, became the darling of the all-rounders, going Reserve Best in Show at Birmingham National and Best in Show at Bath after winning his first two CCs. He was handled by the Tonkins' daughter, Yolanda, and he was a great showman, eventually making up under the American judge Dr Burke. From this early success, the Tonkins started to build up a winning line under the Tonantron banner. They used Glory Boy on Prize Guy's sister and this gave them Ch. Tonantron Glory Girl, who also had a CC-winning brother. Glory Girl was then mated to the Wildmans' Dutch import, Quibus van Rusticana, to produce Ch. Tonantron True Glory for the home kennel and Ch. Tonantron All Glory who went to Wildax. True Glory became a top winner for the kennel, picking up more than 20 CCs, but much more important was one of his early matings to the Tonkins'

Cock Robin daughter, Bella Dora, who whelped a litter, on July 24th 1989, which contained a flashy red and white bitch called Glory Lass. The rest, as they say, is history. I remember going to the Scottish Boxer Club in 1990 and watching Glory Lass sweep through to the Bitch CC at just eight months of age – she was quite stunning and, even at such a young age, she had that startling showmanship which she was famous for. In subsequent years, she won everything there was to win – the breed record with 52 CCs, the record for the most CCs won in a year, Champion of Champions over and over again, Boxer of the Year, many Top Boxer awards and a couple of Best in Show all-breeds. The list is endless, and those of us who had the privilege of seeing her in her prime will never forget her!

TRYWELL
Angela Kennett
A 21st birthday present started this line back in 1957 and Angela's first serious winner, Makreen Man o' War, followed soon after. He had been purchased from Dr McKellar's famous kennel and he won a couple of CCs in the early 60s. Moving into the 1970s, Angela had two puppies back from bitches of her breeding – both were smart red and white dogs, and one was by Picasso and the other was by a Rytonways dog. It is always difficult campaigning two similar Boxers at the same time, but Angela made both Tremendous of Trywell and Thunderbolt of Trywell into Champions. To add to the excitement, Tremendous was Best of Breed at Crufts under Marian Fairbrother in 1974.

However, it was the Picasso son, Thunderbolt, who proved the better sire,

With 21 CCs, Ch. Trywell Twelfth Night is Angela Kennett's most successful Boxer to date.
Photo: Holley.

producing the next three Champions that Angela campaigned: Ch. Alldane Golden Wonder of Trywell and Ch. Alldane Golden Joy of Trywell in partnership with the Duncans, and Ch. Alldane Golden Topper of Trywell in partnership with Shirley Blackley. It was with Shirley that Angela also made up Ch. Think Big of Trywell, who was the result of a Thunderbolt son mated to a Tremendous daughter. In the meantime, Angela had acquired a bitch called Brigadoon Tigermoth who did win a CC, but it was when she was mated to Night Rider that her true worth became clear. Her daughter, Ch. Trywell Twelfth Night, went on to be the biggest winner for Angela, picking up 21 CCs, as well as Reserve Best in Show all-breeds at the

Bred by Sheila Cartwright, Ch. Tyegarth Blue Kiwi won very well for Vince and Annabel Zammit. Blue Kiwi was a son of the great Sive Ch. Tyegarth Famous Grouse.
Photo: Pearce.

Welsh Kennel Club in 1986 under Gwen Broadley. Today, Angela has a smart brindle dog in the ring who recently won his first CC.

TYEGARTH
Sheila Cartwright
Many world-class dogs in a number of different breeds bear the Tyegarth prefix, and Sheila must rank as one of the cleverest dog breeders in the country. Her greatest success in Boxers came with the Summer Storm son, Ch. Tyegarth Famous Grouse, who won a creditable number of CCs in the ring before he set about becoming an all-time great. No sire in the history of the breed has sons and daughters who have won more CCs between them, and among his children are 17 English Champions and many well-known names from Ch. Faerdorn Pheasant Plucker to Ch. Norwatch Slightly Sozzled. Grouse also produced very well for the home kennel, and I remember a succession of his lovely daughters Wee Dram, Gin 'n' Cin, and Brainduster who all became Champions,

together with the male Ch. Tyegarth Blue Kiwi, who won 24 CCs for the Zammits.

To this day, Sheila retains a keen and abiding interest in breeding and she is always willing to try something new. Both American and Dutch imports have been successfully incorporated into the modern Tyegarth line which is still producing Champions. I always value my conversations with Sheila enormously, as she never fails to come up with an interesting thought or a new angle on a potential breeding programme, and you can often look at what she is doing with her own Boxers and think "I wonder why Sheila is doing that?", before it becomes crystal-clear in future generations of her line when the next major winners pop up.

WALKON
Walker and Yvonne Miller
Based in distant Stranraer, the Millers started showing their Boxers at the end of the 1970s and, since that time, they have not looked back, with more than ten English Champions already carrying the Walkon affix. Ch. Jenroy Pop My Cork to Walkon was their first major winner, picking up 21 CCs, Group successes, Champion of Champions and many Top Boxer titles. However, perhaps even more remarkable is the fact that Pop My Cork's last two CCs came out of the Veteran classes. The first at Crufts, no less, and the second at the Irish Boxer Club when he was 10 years of age.

At the same time as they were showing Pop My Cork, the Millers also made up Ch. Slightly Sloshed of Sunhawk at Walkon, who was a Best in Show winner at the British Boxer Club, and they had the Glenmorangie daughter, Ch. Walkon Smash'd Again, who was to prove a most important foundation for them. Clever breeding, and the inclusion of some Dutch blood through Dolf the Buhe Farm of Marbelton, continued the Millers' success and gave them another crop of Champions in the early 90s. During this time, they had also exported a dog and a bitch to Australia. Aust. Ch. Walkon Skittles became a great Specialty winner and Jenroy Pop Back to Walkon proved an excellent stud dog.

On a subsequent trip to Australia, Walker and Yvonne decided that they could do with some more of this breeding back home, and they purchased a dog puppy from Mark Johnston out of the mating between Skittles and Pop Back. The dog was called Blueprint Beern Skittles at Walkon and, at his second show out of quarantine when he was not much more than a puppy, I had the pleasure of awarding this excellent Boxer the Reserve CC. He quickly became a Champion, and in 1995 and 1996 he was the top winning Boxer in the country, with Group successes too. He is now proving useful as a stud dog and the Millers have already made his son, Crocodiledun Dee, into a Champion.

WINUWUK
Marion and Ivor Ward-Davies, Julie Brown and Tim Hutchings
This famous line was started by Marion and Ivor Ward-Davies in the 1950s and, over the years, the Winuwuks have won over 100 CCs. A critical factor in this success was the decision to import Kreyons Back in Town of Winuwuk and then Winuwuk Milray's Red Baron of Valvay – two American dogs who both became top sires and who are behind many of the big names in Boxers, including several for the home

kennel. Ch. Kinbra Uncle Sam of Winuwuk, who won 13 CCs, was by Back in Town; Ch. Winuwuk Good Golly who won 25 was by Baron out of a Back in Town daughter; and Ch. Winuwuk Heaven Forbid was out of a Baron daughter.

In the late 1980s, the kennel acquired from Maureen Best Ch. Wrencliff Flying Scotchman of Winuwuk as a five-month-old puppy. Scotchman was by Brock Buster out of the Baron daughter Ch. Wrencliff Let's Try Again and he proved to be an invaluable purchase. He was a good winner himself with 10 CCs and a Championship show Group, but it is through his daughter that he will be best remembered. Ch. Roamaro Scotch Mist of Winuwuk was bred by Mandy Laidlaw out a Jenroy bitch, and she arrived at Winuwuk in December 1991. In 1992 she was the Top Boxer Puppy, and from 1993 to 1996 she was the top winning Boxer bitch, being Top Boxer in 1993 and 1994. She also won the Boxer of the Year title in 1996, a couple of Groups, Reserve Best in Show all-breeds at the LKA under the famous American judge, Annie Clark, and she is the current British Boxer Club Champion of Champions. With a final total of 35 CCs, she easily took the record from Good Golly as the top winning brindle bitch of all time, as well as Storm's record as the top winning brindle. She is now proving herself as a dam, with Champion, CC and Reserve CC-winning progeny from just two litters to date. Her brother, Roamaro Scot Free of Winuwuk, was also a CC winner and he has sired Champions, so Scotchman's influence continues and the latest Winuwuk Champion, Jubilation, is out of one of his daughters. The Winuwuks were the UK's top Boxer breeders in 1996 and 1997.

Ch. Ymar Admiral of the Fleet.

Photo: Banks.

BEST OF THE REST

To conclude our review of the modern UK Boxer scene, it would be unfair not to have a quick look at some of the other names who continue to make the competition in the English rings so tough. The South West has always been a hotbed of breed enthusiasm. Brenda Groves has had a couple of nice Champions and one near-miss; the brother-and-sister team of John Cormack and Veronica Feaver have just made up their second Champion under the Sugarwood banner; the Rustars have just done the same; and so have Mary Foan's Ymars. Further North, Suzanne and Sandra Carter have produced a couple of good Susancar Champions and they have some good young stock coming through. Janet Weall has had two nice Champion bitches under her Janbeau affix; and, in Liverpool, the Wildmans have had several Champions and CC winners, including the imported Bandelero daughter, Dinneke.

A little further North and West, Angela Harper has recently done very well with her Huttonvales, who have won many CCs in the last couple of years. Over to the North East, Janice Bracher has had a couple of

ABOVE: Ch. Shiloh Doodlebug.

LEFT: Ch. Gypendale Quincy Dental for Susancar.

very good Mulbraes, including two titleholders. Moving down the A1, Stuart Lockwood-Brown and Tony Curtin have so far made up two bitches, including Ch. Shiloh Doodlebug who has done the Boxer proud in the Group, and in Bedfordshire, Ann Podmore is celebrating her second male Champion at Dallgerry. In addition, there are many, many more who make the going tough: David Webb's Cherrysides; the Grahams' Valabeaus; Edna Woods' Sandynes; Wendy Brooks' Jinnybrux; Lynette Davey's Kitwes; Denise Mastaglio's Alexvals; Isobel Edison's Vizages; the Thorpes' Bruliz; Mandy Laidlaw's Roamaros; and the Pyes' Burndens.

UK RECORD BREAKERS
In all walks of life, there is a fascination with records and this is especially true in the world of dogs. However, on a number of recent occasions, I have seen it stated in print by some very well-known exhibitors that trying to break records should not be the aim of true dog breeders. The argument goes that the real enthusiast should never want to achieve supremacy in the ring with

one dog, but should rather want to bring out good young stock on a regular basis to be campaigned for a while and then left at home, except for special occasions.

I am not at all sure that I go along with this point of view. Personally, I love seeing great Boxers in the ring and I believe that their presence sets the standard for everyone else to aim at. This is definitely true in the UK, where up and coming dogs have to beat all the current Champions to win their own titles. I am absolutely certain that it is the record holders who provide all breeders with their burning ambition – we all want to breed the next Picasso or the next Glory Lass – and it is the healthy competition within the breed which keeps us on our mettle. We all know that to produce the best we have to work hard at our breeding programmes, to condition and train our Boxers correctly, and to battle it out in the ring against a lot of other breeders who are doing the same. Competition in so many fields, from athletics to engineering, rocket science to horse racing, has the direct effect of raising standards and extending the boundaries of achievement. Long may it

One of the many Wardrobes 'doubles', achieved on this occasion under Fred Cross with mother and son. Connie is handling the bitch CC winner, Ch. Wardrobes Miss Mink, and the American handler Ben Burwell has the dog CC winner, Ch. Wardrobes Wild Mink.

continue! None of the following records was broken easily, and I make no apologies for celebrating the very best in British Boxers.

TOP KENNEL

The most successful kennels ever were the Wardrobes Boxers, owned by Constance and Wilson Wiley. Everything about Wardrobes was remarkable, and their story is the stuff that blockbuster novels and Hollywood movies are made of. In her youth, Connie was a keen and successful horsewoman and her first husband used to breed hunters and play polo. This marriage lasted seven years, as did her second, after which she married Wilson in a 1940 registry office ceremony where his father refused to sign the register, disapproving of "this dreadful woman" who was marrying his son. Connie often used to relate this story with some amusement: "I think of people's families today, all living with somebody else and no-one thinks a thing about it, but it was all very different in the 40s!" Perhaps it would have seemed that little bit more acceptable if their families had known then that this third marriage would last nearly 60 years and would see both Connie and Wilson well into their nineties.

Wilson's own background was fairly unique for, although he went on to become a distinguished solicitor, his first love was acting and he pursued this with some success during his University days. These were the heady 'Brideshead Revisited' years between the wars, and Wilson was a leading light in the Oxford University Dramatic Society where an excerpt from one review in his scrapbook says it all: "Mr Temple Abady and Mr Wilson Wiley arrived after the interval to send us home fairly aglow with the intoxication of music and merriment. Together, these two artists are irresistible. They have brought their turns at the piano to a pitch which can scarcely be less than perfection." Critical reviews do not come much better than that!

In 1948, eight years after their marriage, the Wileys acquired their first Boxer and it was Connie's keen interest in horses which had attracted her to the breed. She always maintained that the lines of the two animals were similar, and she considered the Boxer to be the hunter that you could bring indoors. Their first two Boxers did not achieve great success in the ring, but when Wilson bought Connie a red bitch for Christmas in 1950 their luck changed. This bitch became their first Champion, Ch. Wardrobes Alma of Greenovia, with the Wardrobes prefix being taken from the delightful hamlet near Princes Risborough where they lived, and which was allegedly one of twelve farms given to Queen Anne in 1709 to pay for her wardrobe. It was in this tiny village – first at a house called Little Wardrobes and then over the road in Upper Wardrobes – that the Wileys' greatest years in Boxers were spent.

Soon after Alma, the Wileys acquired some invaluable breeding on the advice of Dibbie Somerfield (Panfield Boxers) and Marian Fairbrother (Gremlin Boxers). Dibbie persuaded them to buy the Ch. Panfield Ringleader daughter, Wardrobes Gay Taffeta, and Marian encouraged the purchase of Starlight of Belfoyne, who was by Ch. Winkinglight Viking. With this foundation stock, the Wileys never looked back. In June 1995 Wilson told me: "We went about dog showing in a very professional way and we were helped enormously by Eric Fitch Dalglish, the Dachshund expert – he lived nearby and was one of the greatest people ever in dogs. We were terribly lucky to have him as a friend."

The breeding programme which the Wileys and Eric Dalglish pursued resulted in a string of glorious Champions with tremendous style. It was essentially a programme of very close line-breeding and in-breeding, with many Champions coming from brother-sister and father-daughter matings. The closeness of the Wileys' breeding caused much comment within the breed and, for a while, earned them the nickname of the 'clueless Wileys'. However, their critics were very swiftly silenced and Wardrobes was the undisputed top kennel for the sixteen years from 1956 to 1971, dramatically upgrading the quality of UK Boxers. In total, 427 Boxers carried the famous affix and it is remarkable that 31 of these became UK Champions with another 20-plus overseas. At home, their dogs won

217 CCs and 136 RCCs in the twenty-five years that Connie and Wilson were showing and, among these, there were several outstanding winners, including the great Ch. Wardrobes Miss Mink who, with four all-breed Best in Shows to her name, remains the most successful Boxer ever in all-breed competition. In the breed ring, Mink was only beaten once in her class and this was by her sister, Ch. Wardrobes Miss Sable.

However, just as dramatically as Wardrobes had burst on to the show scene, the end also came abruptly. In the autumn of 1973, Connie was showing Ch. Wardrobes Clair de Lune, who was then the breed record holder with 31 CCs. She was placed third and, it is said, the judge openly expressed the view that, although she thought Clair was in fact the best in the class, she would have to place her down the line to give someone else a chance! Connie felt that she was being pegged back, due to her past successes, and she walked out of the ring that day, never to return. However, although the Wileys stopped showing, they remained leading figures in the canine world. Wilson had a very distinguished history of service to the Kennel Club, they both continued to judge regularly, and you often saw them at the British Boxer Club Shows (where Connie was patron) and at the lovely Summer Championship Show in Windsor.

Until 1995 they stayed remarkably well and continued to live at their magical Upper Wardrobes home, with its classic English outlook, but they eventually had to move down to a Hampshire retirement home where, in 1997, Wilson died at the age of 94. With his outstanding legal career, his unparalleled service as the Clerk to the

Worshipful Company of Founders (a 600-year-old City of London Livery Company), and his lifetime of achievement in dogs, he earned glowing obituaries in the national press. His life was celebrated in a memorial service at St Bartholomew the Great in the heart of the City. Then, only a few short weeks after she had sparkled at this memorial service, Connie also died at the age of 96 – bringing the whole story full circle and reuniting her with her beloved Wilson. The records set by the Wileys in the Boxer ring are now legend and, to this day, no kennel comes close to taking the Wardrobes crown. A couple of years back, I had the great honour of interviewing the Wileys at Upper Wardrobes and I shall forever remember their grace and their style which remained completely undimmed by the passing of years.

Ch. Seefeld Picasso, the record-breaking Boxer sire, pictured during a 1971 show campaign in Ireland where he was Top Dog all breeds.
Photo: O'Carroll.

TOP SIRE

Ch. Wardrobes Miss Sable, who earned a mention in the Wardrobes tale, was actually owned by Monica Norrington of the Radden Boxers and, following the trend of in-breeding set so successfully by the Wileys, Sable was eventually mated to her full brother, Ch. Wardrobes Red Sash. This was in the late 1950s and one of the resulting puppies, Radden Rosina, was bought by Pat Heath as foundation stock for her new Seefeld kennel. Rosina was eventually mated to Wardrobes Delhart's Mack The Knife, who had been imported from the United States by Connie and Wilson. Pat Heath kept a smart red and white bitch from the litter who made up into Ch. Seefeld Musk Rose – the first in a long line of Seefeld bitch Champions. Musk Rose was then mated to Pat's first Champion, Ch. Seefeld Holbein. The

resulting litter was a bit of a disappointment with four plain puppies arriving first, followed by an oddly-marked biscuit-coloured male, who had an off-putting white wedge between his eyes and a large black patch stretching from the middle of his back right down to his knee. Pat took one look at him in the nest and thought that Musk Rose might as well not have bothered!

However, Pat ended up keeping the dog because she wanted to retain the breeding, and she did not know whether she would be able to mate Musk Rose again because she had broken her back as a puppy. There is a moral in this story for all of us because, as the puppy grew, it soon became very apparent that he had star quality. The black patch on his back all but disappeared and his colour deepened to a lovely red. On top of this, he had showmanship to die for.

This dog was the outstanding International Ch. Seefeld Picasso, who must be the greatest all-round achiever the UK breed has ever seen. It was as a show dog that he first caught the imagination, with 24 CCs coupled with much success in all-breed competition where he picked up five Groups, two Reserve Best in Shows, and one Best in Show at the big general Championship Shows. He was also runner-up in the Working Group at Crufts in 1972, the year after he had been the top show dog all-breeds in Southern Ireland. However, it is as a sire that he earns his place in the hall of fame, producing winner after winner to a very wide range of bloodlines, indicating true dominance as a stud dog. Picasso produced 18 UK Champions and another 12 CC or RCC winners. Among these was Ch. Calidad Bright Boots, whom many consider was one of the nicest Boxer bitches ever to be shown in the UK.

As a postscript to the Picasso story, it is worth mentioning that his parents, Musk Rose and Holbein, were both born at exactly the same time on exactly the same day, December 17th 1962 – perhaps they were destined to produce such an important Boxer. Coincidence or fate?

A REMARKABLE FAMILY OF RECORD HOLDERS

Our final set of record breakers all have very close connections, so I will take them as a family group and consider their extraordinary successes in chronological order.

Marian Fairbrother ranks as one of the most knowledgeable dog breeders the country has ever seen. She was there right at the start of the Boxer breed, laying the foundations upon which many other kennels have been built, and at the time of her death she was still making up Champions. In 1974, she mated her good-producing stud dog, Gremlin Famous

Footsteps, to Gremlin Mere Magic. This mating combined the best of the American bloodlines which Marian had introduced to the UK with the American imports Rainey Lane Sirrocco and Treceder's Catch Me Red. Born in January 1975 by Caesarean section, the resulting litter of seven contained a brindle and white dog puppy who was to become Ch. Gremlin Summer Storm, widely acknowledged as one of the

Marian Fairbrother's Ch. Gremlin Summer Storm, one-time record holder, who remains the top winning brindle male.

best-made and soundest-moving Boxers ever. Summer Storm quickly notched up an impressive collection of tickets and, with 33, he held the breed record at the time of his owner's death. This record may have now fallen, but he remains the **Top Male CC winner of all time.** His long-term influence on the breed has also been profound, and his own tally of seven Champion children is worth mentioning, but what is more important is that among these are his two sons, Ch. Tyegarth Glenmorangie of Jenroy and Ch. Tyegarth Famous Grouse, both of whom became great sires. Indeed, Famous Grouse came within a whisker of taking Picasso's record as the breed's top producer but, although his children actually won a few more CCs than Picasso's, Grouse sired one less Champion. It was a photo-finish!

Summer Storm's full sister was a bitch called Gremlin Semi Sweet, whom Marian eventually mated back to Famous Footsteps, her father. It was from this litter that Helen Watchorn (later Banks) bought a bitch puppy called Gremlin Soft Steps who, in turn, produced the foundation of the Norwatch Kennel, the reserve CC-winning Norwatch Mustang Wine who will always be remembered through her offspring. When she was mated to Bruce Cattanach's dominant stud dog, Ch. Steynmere Nightrider, she produced Ch. Norwatch Brock Buster, Ch. Norwatch Glory Boy of Rayfos, and Ch. Norwatch O'Toole of Rayfos. Then, to Famous Grouse, she produced Ch. Norwatch Slightly Sozzled and Ch. Slightly Sloshed of Sunhawk at Walkon. Mustang Wine's five UK Champions who won 57 CCs and 49 RCCs make her, with some margin, the **Top Dam of all time** and her family continued to breed on successfully.

Her red son, Glory Boy, owned by Barbara and Philip Greenway, was a successful stud dog and in 1982 he produced a red male for the Greenways who was an instant hit in the show ring. Ch. Rayfos Cockrobin gained his title out of Junior and he picked up 26 CCs in total, which gave him the **Red Male record** from Picasso. Robin was a tremendously popular dog within the breed and such a good Boxer overall. I well remember watching him go Best of Breed at Crufts in 1985 and winning the very first Boxer of the Year finals later that same year.

Norwatch Mustang Wine collecting the Dam of Merit trophy from Stafford Somerfield of the Panfield Boxers.

For a while, there were some PA implications lurking way back in Cock Robin's pedigree so he was not widely used at stud. However, the Tonkins did put their Glory Boy daughter to him and this produced Tonantron Bella Dora. Bella Dora was then mated to their own Ch. Tonantron True Glory, who was a Glory Boy grandson. If you follow this through logically, you will realise that the resulting puppies are very heavily line-bred on Glory Boy, who appears on their pedigree as the great grandsire in three out of the four possible positions. One of the puppies from this litter turned out to be the sensational red bitch, Ch. Tonantron Glory Lass, who had smashed Storm's breed record by the age of three and finished up with 52 CCs and a shedful of other wins along the way. Philip Greenway often handled her and, deservedly, she had a very large fan club, reflecting her status as the **breed record holder.** She was a magnificent Boxer and an

Best in Show winner at the 50th anniversary show of the British Boxer Club, Ch. Rayfos Cockrobin, is the top winning red male of all time.   Photo: Hartley.

After winning her first CC at eight months of age, Ch. Tonantron Glory Lass became the breed record holder by the age of three. Photo: Broughton.

immaculate show girl.

In the meantime Glory Boy's brother, Ch. Norwatch Brock Buster had sired the group winning Ch. Wrencliff Flying Scotchman of Winuwuk. Flying Scotchman was then put to a bitch called Jenroy Popsicle for Belmont who was also a member of the family, being a grand-daughter of Glenmorangie on father's side and of Brock Buster on mother's. This litter produced

Ch. Norwatch Brock Buster started a record breaking line of Champions for the Norwatch Sunhawk kennel   Photo: Holley.

Ch. Roamaro Scotch Mist of Winuwuk who was bred by Mandy Laidlaw and owned by Marion and Ivor Ward-Davies, Julie Brown and myself. Scotch Mist's show career took off immediately and, as Glory Lass entered retirement, Misty took over the bitch challenges and picked up a total of 35 CCs. This makes her the **top brindle Boxer ever and the runner-up of all time.**

The recent dominance of this family of Boxers, which stretches back to the old Gremlin breeding, is almost incredible and within it is also the **record-breaking line of direct Champions** which has been established by Helen and Eddie Banks. A few other kennels have achieved a creditable line of titleholders, but none can match the seven at Norwatch-Sunhawk, which stretch back to Ch. Norwatch Brock Buster. I find it encouraging that, of the eight major records which I have highlighted, six have been established since 1980. This indicates to me that the breed is progressing strongly and I think it is an entirely healthy state of affairs when records are continually refreshed and exceeded. I look forward to seeing this trend continue into the next millennium.

12 BOXERS IN NORTH AMERICA

I have been a very keen follower of the North American show scene for a number of years and have attended many shows since my first trip to the 50th Anniversary celebrations of the American Boxer Club. This show attracted getting on for 900 exhibits and included a parade of nearly 300 Champions. I was struck by the

sheer professionalism of the dog scene, and it was wonderful to see the rapport which the great handlers had with their dogs. But, perhaps above everything else, I was most impressed by the temperament and showmanship of the exhibits. The Boxers came into the ring, preened their elegant necks, stood up on their toes without

A unique photo showing seven Best of Breed winners from past American Boxer Club National and Regional Specialty shows. From left to right: Ch. Salgray's Ambush handled by Stan Flowers; Ch. Kreyon's Firebrand with Margaret Krey; Ch. Arriba's Prima Donna and Ch. Salgray's Double Talk with Jane Forsyth; Dick Baum handling Ch. Nadora's Black Lace; Alvin Lee showing Ch. Yours True Lee; and Ch. Scher-Khoun's Shadrack being shown by his owner-breeder, Shirley De Boer.

showing a shred of aggression and moved with tremendous presence. On top of all this, there was an impressive uniformity of type, and I was lucky that some of the best Boxers in recent history were either just at the start of their careers or were already in their prime. As a showcase of world-class Boxers, this event took some beating, and I will remember it for a very long time.

On subsequent trips, I am pleased to say that I have continued to see a large number of really outstanding show dogs and there is no doubt in my mind that some of the best-ever Boxers have been North American. The Americans can also teach the rest of us a thing or two about conditioning dogs and presenting them in the ring. The handlers are true professionals, who have a real understanding of what makes the breed tick, and there is no country in the world where Boxers are shown so effectively. Watching the likes of Kim Pastella, Gary Steele, Marylou Hatfield and the Baums taking their special dogs into the ring is an education and a pleasure. But it is the breeders who produce the dogs in the first place, and in this chapter we take a look at some of the kennels which are currently enjoying their fair share of show ring successes.

ARRIBA
Ted Fickes
Nahum's Arriba was the foundation of this well-known kennel in 1964. She was never shown, but she produced a couple of Champions and got the line off to a good start. The kennel's best-known winner was the outstanding bitch Ch. Arriba's Prima Donna who went Best in Show all-breeds on 23 occasions, including the Westminster Show in 1970 where she won through the

breed under the celebrated British breeder and judge, Wilson Wiley.

Well over 50 Champions have carried the Arriba name, and the kennel has also produced ten Sires and Dams of Merit which is quite an achievement. One year at the American Boxer Club, three Arriba Champions, Prima Donna, Castanet and Calypso, were all competing in the Winners Bitch class and this remains one of Ted Fickes' proudest memories. On a recent trip to America, I was pleased to see that the Arriba name is still very much to the fore, thanks to the current successes of Ch. Arriba Talisman Ego, handled by Michael Shepherd for Cheryl and Keith Robbins. I also much admired the excellent heads on the very good Champions, Ch. Talisman Arriba Silverado and Ch. Arriba Talisman Epitome.

CAYMAN
Sydney Brown
Sydney bought her first Boxer in 1953, but it was not until 1985, when she bought her foundation bitch, Ch. El Sirrah's Cayman Gold, that she started exhibiting seriously. This bitch proved to be a wonderful purchase, becoming a Dam of Merit from her first litter. In total, she produced five American Champions and one Canadian Champion, along with a couple of bitches who became Dams of Merit in their own right. Cayman Gold's progeny included Ch. Cayman's Mac Scott and Ch. Cayman's Dapper Dan, who were Group Winners, and Ch. Cayman's Sweet Nandi who went on to produce the lovely brindle male, Ch. Cayman's Black Bart. I am a real fan of Black Bart who won the American Boxer Club Top Twenty in 1995. He is a really well-made dog with a lovely outline, and he

Ch. Cayman's Mac Scott winning a Group.
Photo: Cook.

won the award from a very high-powered panel of judges consisting of Harriet Campbell, Eleanor Linderholm-Wood and Christine Baum.

Currently, the kennel is doing very well with Ch. Cayman's Texas Ranger who is among the top ten winning Boxers in America. I also recently saw Gary Steele showing one of Sydney's young dogs who really caught my eye. He is called Nightrider and I was pleased to hear from Sydney, when I last spoke with her, that he has now become a Champion. Like so many breeders, Sydney's number one priority is the health of her stock and their temperament.

CHERKEI
Keith and Cheryl Robbins
This Georgia-based kennel has been turning out Champions of great quality for longer than its owners will care to remember. To date, well over 50 titleholders have carried

the Cherkei name, including some big winners in the 1990s show rings. Ch. Cherkei's High Cotton was born in 1989, sired by the great Ch. Golden Haze Tuxedo out of the Dam of Merit, Ch. Cherkei's Arriba Wicked Calita. He quickly established a reputation and was the number three Boxer in 1991 and 1992.

In due course, Cotton was mated to TuRo's Miata who was a daughter of the great sire Ch. Marquam Hills Traper of TuRo. This was an interesting piece of line breeding and it produced Ch. Cherkei's Ultimate High, who was the second top winning Boxer in the USA for 1995 and 1996. As Cheryl Robbins says: "Just occasionally, it is nice to have fabulous luck with a breeding. Cotton to Mia looked great on paper and the strengths and weaknesses matched well, but none of us ever expected the breathtaking, spine-tingling puppy that resulted." The Robbinses are tremendously proud of Ultimate High, who has now sired five Champions, and I must say that I was impressed by him when I saw him competing in the recent Top Twenty contest. For 1997, Cherkei are showing the beautifully headed red dog, Ch. Arriba Talisman Ego, who is presently running third Top Boxer.

CROSSROADS
Marshall and Dorothy Hart and family
While Marshall Hart was in hospital, recovering from heart surgery, Dorothy and their daughter purchased the foundation of the Crossroads kennel. Their first litter produced Champions and others soon followed, including Ch. Crossroad's Movin' On Up, who was the Grand Futurity winner at the Boxer Nationals. As they were

starting their breeding programme, the Harts were fortunate to have Paul Van Sinden as a mentor and friend. Sadly, Paul died soon after Crossroads had won their first Best of Breed, but the kennel honoured him when they named their most successful litter to date, which contained Ch. Crossroads PVS On My Honour, Ch. Crossroads PVS Tribute and Ch. Crossroads PVS Remembered. This litter was sired by that great red Boxer male, Ch. Heldenbrand's Jet Breaker, and On My Honour is an all-breed Best in Show winner. He also won an Award of Merit at the 1997 Westminster show and was a Top Twenty contender.

The Harts often say to themselves that they have been very lucky to have been so successful in such a short space of time but, having spent many years with several different types of livestock, they believe that to produce quality animals you have to start with something good, latch on to a willing mentor – and listen. The success of the Crossroads kennel is testament to this philosophy.

CYNRA
Beatrice Wade
Thirteen litters have been bred by the Cynra kennels, and 22 Champions have been owned by Beatrice Wade, who started out in the breed back in 1956. Early success was achieved and Ch. Cynra's Star Trek was Winners Dog at Westminster in 1978. However, the kennel's main priority has always been to produce good bitches who breed on. Recently, Beatrice has had a couple of outstanding Dams of Merit, including Ch. Cynra's Chanel, who is owned in partnership with the Truesdales. Chanel was mated to Ch. Hi-Tech's

Arbitrage and this resulted in three Champions. She was then mated to the Arbitrage son Ch. Hi-Tech's Aristocrat and produced another three titleholders, with more in the litter who could yet finish. In her breeding programme, Beatrice likes to put her bitches to a variety of stud dogs, even if earlier litters have been outstanding. This is because she believes that, if a bitch produces successfully to one dog, then she is likely to do the same to a different sire. I must say that I share Beatrice's belief in this, especially if the bitch herself is bred to produce.

ELHARLEN
Eleanor and Harold Foley
This Canadian line started with a double grand-daughter of the legendary Ch. Bang Away of Sirrah Crest, but its foundation bitch was Ch. Bobby Pin of Blossomlea, sired by the famous Ch. Salgray's Flying High. She did not really care for the ring, but Bobby Pin more than made up for this in the whelping box where she became the dam of many Champions. One of the Foleys' most memorable experiences was when the Hamilburgs, owners of the Salgray Boxers, sent their great handler, Larry Downey, to Canada in order to buy two dog puppies from the Elharlen kennels. For the Foleys, listening to Larry's stories of the early Boxers in the US and war-time Germany was the greatest thrill. One of the puppies which Larry purchased, Ch. Salgray's Double Talk, went Best of Breed at the American Boxer Club, and standing reserve to him was his other purchase, Ch. Salgray's Double Play, who was Double Talk's brother! During this same visit, Larry also purchased Elharlen's Cameo who was by Ch. Salgray's Fashion Plate. She was

then bred to Ch. Salgray's Ovation to produce Ch. Galanjud's Blue Chip, who was also a BOB winner at the ABC in the year Pat Heath from the UK was judging.

Over the years, the Foleys have produced many outstanding Boxers. Ch. Elharlen's Opening Knight was Canada's Top Boxer Puppy one year and runner-up to the Top Boxer. Ch. Elharlen's Illusive Dream and Ch. Elharlen's Quixotical were also big winners. Bringing things right up to date, Ch. Elharlen's The Yachtsman was in the American Boxer Club Top Twenty in 1996 and 1997, and Ch. Elharlen's Your Choice is one of the current top winners in Canada. All of these successes have made the Foleys the Top Breeders in Canada on four occasions. They remain eternally grateful to Jean Grant for letting them buy Bobby Pin, and to Phyllis Hamilburg who taught Eleanor that it is easy to fault a dog, but it takes a keen eye and a wise breeder to assess the whole animal.

HI-TECH
Bill and Tina Truesdale

I have long been an admirer of the Hi-Tech Boxers, who have rapidly established a formidable reputation with a succession of impressive Champions and, more particularly, a famous direct line of four red Champion males. Ch. Fiero's Tally Ho Tailo was a serious winner in breed and all-breed competition and he was a most important sire for Bill and Tina, producing more than 10 Champions for the home kennel as well as many more for other breeders. One of Tailo's sons, Ch. Hi-Tech's Arbitrage, was the Top Twenty winner in 1992, Best of Breed at the American Boxer Club in 1994 and Best Opposite at the 50th anniversary show in 1993. In 1994 he was also the Top

ABOVE:. The magnificent Ch. Hi-Tech's Arbitrage ... just perfect!

Photo: Ashbey.

BELOW: Ch. Hi-Tech's Aristocrat, a son of Arbitrage and an excellent stud dog.

Photo: Marcia.

Ch. Hi-Tech's Johnny J of Boxerton, a son of Ch. Hi-Tech's Aristocrat, handled by Kimberly Pastella. Photo: Ashbey.

Boxer in the USA and the number one working dog in the country. In addition, he is now one of America's leading sires. Arbitrage is my favourite Boxer of all time. When I saw him last, winning the Veteran class at the 1997 American Boxer Club, all one of my Australian friends could say was "He's just perfect," and I agree with her wholeheartedly. The Arbitrage son Ch. Hi-Tech's Aristocrat has now produced on well for the Truesdales. He sired Ch. Hi-Tech's Johnny J of Boxerton, who is out of an Arbitrage daughter, for them. Johnny was Best of Breed at the 1996 ABC Regional and then again at the 1997 Nationals under John Connolly. The Hi-Tech kennels are based in Massachusetts and their Boxers are piloted by Kimberly Pastella. There have been dozens of Hi-Tech Champions already

and few would doubt that there will be many more in the future.

HOLLY LANE
Eileen McClintock

The first Holly Lane Champion, Cookie, was produced in the second litter bred at the kennel, when Eileen put a daughter of Ch. Jered's Spellbinder to Ch. Flintwoods Sundowner. Ch. Holly Lane's Cookie was subsequently mated to Ch. Brayshaws Masquerader and the result was the famous 'Wind' litter, which contained the Sire of Merit, Ch. Holly Lane's Wildwind, along with Ch. Holly Lane's Wind Snow and Ch. Holly Lane's Wind Siren. However, the most famous littermate was the Group-winning red bitch, Ch. Holly Lane's Windstorm, who went on to produce a record-breaking total of 11 American Champions, eight of which were sired by the famous producer Ch. Scher-Khouns Meshack. The stream of Champions has continued, and I saw my first Holly Lane Champion at the 1993 American Boxer Club, when the beautiful Ch. Holly Lane's Free as the Wind won the Futurity – she certainly captured a few English hearts that day!

The Holly Lane name is still there to this day. At the 1997 ABC, Ch. Holly Lane's Baccarat Teohlin won the Stud Dog class for the Federmans, Ch. Holly Lane's Spin a Dream won an Award of Merit, and Eileen McClintock was honoured with the coveted Larry Downey award, recognising her outstanding efforts on behalf of the American Boxer Club.

HUFFAND
Linda and Jerry Huffman and Carole and John Connolly

This partnership started back in the early 1970s and many good Boxers have been produced since then. Early successes came when Ch. Huffands Charade was bred by putting Linda's dog, Ch. Arriba's High Hopes, to Carole's bitch, Arriba's Ultimate. Charade became an important producer of six Champions, including four in her first litter back to her sire. This was the 'H' litter, and the Champions were High Time, High Society, High Test and Highland Fling. Needless to say, the success of her kids made Charade a Dam of Merit, and her mother, Ultimate, earned the same honour.

In 1978, the partnership was presented with the prestigious awards for the Kennel Making and Breeding the Most Champions. A very large number of Champions has been made up by these talented breeders and their name is still out in front. In February 1997, I watched the beautifully headed bitch, Ch. Huffands Obladah of Arriba, win Best Opposite Sex at the Westminster Kennel Club against some stiff opposition.

JACQUET
Rick Tomita and Bill Scolnik
The Jacquet story began in 1968 when Rick and Bill wanted a Boxer as protection for their antique business. The kennel acquired its name from their first dog, Jacquet Droz, who was named after the 18th century French musical clock maker. Since then, over 160 American Champions and 250 Champions worldwide have carried the Jacquet name. Among these are top winners and producers, such as Ch. Happy Ours de Jacquet who has produced over 60 Champions worldwide, and his grand-daughter Ch. Jacquet's Cambridge Fortune who was acclaimed as the Top Boxer Bitch

Ch. Jacquet's Novarese, a Sire of Merit.

in 1994. So far, Jacquet has received the annual award for the Kennel Making the Most Champions 13 times and they have won the award for Breeding the Most Champions 15 times, which is a record.

The multi-titled Ch. Jacquet's Novarese has really progressed the line, and he quickly became a Sire of Merit, but, in the early 1990s, Rick felt it was time to introduce another line to breed with. After much research, he bought a tightly-bred grand-daughter of Ch. TuRo's Cachet called Jacquet's Siren de Goldfield. He put her to the Novarese son Ch. Jacquet's Greggson and, among others, this produced Ch. Jacquet's Bravo of Goldfield who has been in the Top Ten for the last couple of years.

I am proud to call Rick Tomita a friend, and it was my great pleasure to visit his kennels recently and take a look at the next generation of famous Jacquets.

JAEGERHOUSE
Verena Jaeger
This well-known Canadian kennel was established in 1979 and soon became a force to be reckoned with. So far it has bred 65 Canadian Champions and three American Champions, along with several

Ch. Mephisto's Rosenkavalier, the sire of 50 Champions.   *Photo: Linda Lindt.*

Boxers who have acquitted themselves well in Obedience competition. At present, the kennel is doing very well, in the sixth generation of its breeding, with Ch. Jaegerhouse Intrepid Razer who is one of Canada's top Boxers.

JOPA
Joe and Pat Rush

This kennel has been consistently producing some very good Boxers of excellent type from its base in Maryland. Among many good wins, Joe and Pat have enjoyed some exciting successes at the Boxer Nationals. In 1989, they went Reserve Winners with Ch. Jopa's Dr Action and then, in 1992, their red bitch, Ch. Jopa's Smouldering Ember, was awarded Best of Winners. Ember was bred from their Dam of Merit, Ch. Jopa's Weekend Fantasy. Bringing things right up to date, the son of Ch. Golden Haze Tuxedo, Ch. Jopa's Great Gusto of Higos, was handled by Ricky Justice to an Award of Merit in a very hotly contested Best of Breed competition at the 1997 Nationals.

KREYON
Margaret Krey

Margaret Krey has been breeding good Boxers for a very long time. One of the nicest bitches bred by the kennel was Ch. Kreyon's Firebrand, who was sired by Ch. Cajon's Calling Card. Firebrand was the Grand Prize Futurity winner in 1968 and she was Best of Breed at the ABC Regional in the same year. She was also an all-breed Best in Show winner. When Firebrand was mated to that great sire, Ch. Scher-Khoun's Shadrack, she produced Kreyon's Back in Town, who was exported to the Winuwuk kennels in England where he became such an important influence in the development of the modern UK Boxer. Back in Town was used once before he left the Kreyon kennel, and one of his puppies, Rainey-Lane's Grand Slam, was exported to Australia where he sired 19 Champions.

It is interesting, 20 years on, that Margaret has recently exported semen from her current Sire of Merit, Ch. Kreyon's Easy Money, to David and Juanita Strachan in Australia and several good Champions have resulted. The worldwide influence of the Kreyon kennel cannot be doubted, and the Champions still continue at home, such as the Dam of Merit Ch. Kreyon's Delta Dawn II and Ch. Kreyon's Let's Dance, who won the 1997 Junior Futurity.

MEPHISTO
Walter and Monika Pinsker

Ch. Haviland's Gold Rebel was the Pinskers' first Boxer, purchased in 1968, but the true foundation for this Canadian kennel was Ch. Scher-Khoun's Autumn Concerto who produced 10 Champions, including several famous Best in Show winners. Another important brood bitch for the Pinskers was Ch. Verwood's Lollipop, a Fashion Hint daughter. She exceeded all expectations by producing 12 Champions, and among her children was Ch. Mephisto's Soldier of Fortune who was the Top Dog in Canada, siring over 100 Champions along the way.

To this day, the Mephisto name is still up there in lights and the dogs are now handled by the Pinskers' daughter, Michelle. Ch. Mephisto's Rosenkavalier is now an American and Canadian Sire of Merit, with 50 Champions to his credit and his son, Ch. Mephisto's Guns and Roses, was the leading Boxer in 1995 and 1996 and number ten all-breeds.

Jack Ireland handling Ch. Pinepath's Night Watch to a Best in Show.

PINEBROOK
Tom and Arlene Perret
Tom and Arlene have been breeding Boxers for well over 30 years, based at their home in Ohio. In more recent years, Ch. Pinebrook's Innuendo has been a good producer for them. He is a red male out of Ch. Fiero Tally Ho Tailo's sister and sired by Ch. Pinebrook's Well Tailored. Innuendo has quickly gained recognition as a Sire of Merit. In 1995, his son, Ch. Kimber-D Pinebrook Dusty Road, won the ABC National Specialty and was a Top Twenty contender. There have been many nice Champions under this affix and I particularly remember Ch. Pinebrooks Grand Visage, a smart red and white male with a very well-balanced outline.

PINEPATH
Jack and Cathryn Ireland
The Pinepath kennel is based in Canada, where Jack purchased his first show dog in 1963. Since then, he has owned or bred over 100 Canadian or American

Champions. A great winner on both sides of the border for Pinepath was Ch. Greenhavens Ebony at Pinepath, who was the Top Best of Breed Boxer in Canada during 1989. Jack then mated Ebony to the Truesdales' good producer, Ch. Fiero's Tally Ho Tailo, and from this litter came Ch. Pinepaths Night Watch who was Canada's top winning Best in Show puppy during 1990. Night Watch went on to become an excellent sire himself, attaining Sire of Merit status in both America and Canada. I have always followed Night Watch's career closely, and, if ever a well-made, typically headed brindle puppy really catches my eye at a North American show, I often find that Night Watch is somewhere in the pedigree when I look it up. Jack is currently doing well with the Night Watch son, Ch. Cherkei Midnite 'n' Montgomery.

ROCHIL
Sandi and Perry Combest
Since 1973, 10 Champions have been owned or bred by the Rochil kennels. The best-known was undoubtedly Ch. Rochil's

Grande Marshall, a Boxer with an outstanding winning record in the breed and all-breed rings. He was the winner of 23 all-breed Best in Shows and he won the first American Boxer Club Top Twenty competition, in which three of his progeny also competed in subsequent years. Sandi and Perry have owned three Sires or Dams of Merit over the years, and quality Boxers continue to come from this Texas-based kennel.

ROSEND
Jerry and Lynda Yon
This Californian kennel was founded in 1989 when Jerry and Lynda Yon purchased two brindle bitch puppies. Glenroe Brandy 'n' Cream soon became a Champion and High Crest's Desert Rose produced their first homebred Champion, Rosend's Stardust. To strengthen their breeding programme further in the early 1990s, the Yons bought the impressive red male Ch. Bridgewood's B K Kahuna, when he was 16 months old. Campaigned by Gary Steele, he was the number one Boxer on the West Coast in 1993 and 1994. He twice competed at the ABC Top Twenty and has already sired 12 Champions, including several Top Twenty contenders. The Yons have recently done well with Ch. Rosend's Bo Diddley, Ch. Rosend's Uptown Girl and Ch. Rosend's Corporate Raider, all of whom are sired by Kahuna.

RUMMER RUN
Steve and Ann Anderson
In 1978, while living in Texas, Steve and Ann had the opportunity to buy their first two Boxers, Ch. TuRo's Power Play of Box Run and Ch. TuRo's Tearaway of Box Run. Power Play produced their first homebred

Ricky Justice is handling Ch. Rummer-Run's Stardust, the 1997 ABC Top Twenty and Regional Specialty winner.   Photo: Meyer.

Champion and, since then, they have bred another 23 Champions under the Rummer Run banner. They chose their kennel name because one of their early pets was called Rum and, on looking through the dictionary, they noticed that a Rummer is a large victory chalice. When combined with Run, it had a nice ring to it and so the Boxers were duly christened.

In recent years, the Andersons have worked with bloodlines primarily from Ch. Bropats Red Alert, Ch. Shieldmont's Let's Make a Deal, Ch. Hi-Tech's Arbitrage and Ch. Hi-Tech's Aristocrat. This is obviously working for them, since they are currently campaigning some excellent Boxers, including Ch. Rummer Run's Stardust who is being exhibited nationwide with great success. Stardust is by Arbitrage, and I was very pleased to see her win the 1997 Top Twenty. I was most impressed by her stunning outline, excellent forehand and cracking temperament. She then went on to win the American Boxer Club Regional later in the same year.

SIRROCCO
Diane Mallett

The story of this winning kennel started in 1968 when Diane was given a Boxer as a wedding present. This dog was actually a grandson of Rainey-Lane's Sirrocco (the dog eventually imported to the UK by Marian Fairbrother and Martin Summers) and it is from him that the kennel got its name. Diane's first interest was in Obedience training and in providing Service and Assistant dogs for the handicapped, but she soon branched out to try her hand at professionally handling dogs in the ring. After a few years living in Europe, Diane eventually returned to the USA with an American-bred bitch who produced a most important daughter called Sirrocco's Kiss 'n' Tell, owned in partnership with Kathleen Gould.

For her first litter, Kiss 'n' Tell was mated to the outstanding stud dog Ch. Golden Haze Tuxedo, and the resulting puppies quickly became known as the 'dream team'. Ch. Sirrocco's Night's Candles is a group winner and his sister, Ch. Sirrocco's Kiss by the Book, was the winner of the prestigious American Boxer Club Top Twenty competition in 1996. I first saw Kiss by the Book at the famous Westminster show in February 1997 and was immediately struck by her outstanding head and expression. She is a most eye-catching bitch and she is currently running Top Boxer in the USA.

Another member of the dream team, Ch.

Pictured as a puppy, Ch. Sirrocco's Do Applaud is being handled to a Sweepstakes win by her owner, Diane Mallett.
Photo: The Standard Image.

Sirrocco's Far More Fair, was eventually put to Ch. Laurel Hills Evening Star (a son of the famous Ch. Kiebla's Tradition of TuRo) and she produced Ch. Sirrocco's Do Applaud. This bitch really took my fancy when she appeared at the American Boxer Club earlier this year at just seven months of age, and I was absolutely delighted when my good friend David Strachan from Australia made her Reserve Winners Bitch from an entry of 240.

From my own knowledge of the Sirrocco Boxers, it is quite apparent that a prepotent bitch line has been established. Diane Mallett must be delighted that Kiss 'n' Tell recently became a Dam of Merit and even more pleased that her influence continues to be obvious through the generations.

TURO
Sandy Roberts and Elizabeth Esacove

This line was originally established in 1964 by Sandy Roberts and Pat Turner in Oklahoma. It is now based on the TuRo Ranch in Texas, and it must be a contender

Two of the great Boxers which have carried the famous TuRo name, both being rewarded by the acclaimed judge Anne Rogers Clark.

ABOVE: Ch. TuRo's Futurian of Cachet winning Best in Show at the celebrated Santa Barbara Kennel Club. His handler, Gary Steele, considered Futurian to be the best Boxer he had ever presented. *Photo: Bergman.*

BELOW: Ch. Kiebla's Tradition of TuRo winning Best of Breed at the 50th anniversary show of the American Boxer Club. The affinity between 'Tiggin' and her handler, Christine Baum, had to be seen to be believed.
Photo: Ashbey.

for the title of the most successful Boxer kennel ever. TuRo is the owner or breeder of the second top producing Boxer Sire of all time (Ch. Marquam Hills Traper of TuRo), as well as the second and third top winning Boxers of all time (Ch. Kiebla's Tradition of TuRo and Ch. TuRo's Cachet). Furthermore, a TuRo has been the Top Winning Boxer in the USA in 1983, 1984, 1985, 1990, 1991, 1992, 1993, 1995 and 1996, thanks to Cachet, Tradition and Ch. TuRo's Futurian of Cachet.

The TuRo successes really started when one of their foundation bitches, Ch. Hansparke's Fashion Fair, was mated back to her sire, the wonderful producer Ch. Millan's Fashion Hint. This breeding produced Ch. TuRo's Native Dancer who, in turn, became a Sire of Merit producing 18 Champions. The TuRo kennels have continued with their successful line-breeding programme, with occasional in-breeding, and the results speak for themselves, with countless Champions.

I consider myself extremely fortunate to have seen Ch. Kiebla's Tradition of TuRo and Ch. TuRo's Futurian of Cachet exhibited in their prime – both of them are outstanding Boxers and splendid show dogs. The last time I saw Tradition, she was still at the top of the tree, winning Best Opposite at the 1997 ABC from the Veteran class, aged nine – and when 'Tiggin' is in the ring there is not a dry eye in the house. She had previously been BOB at the Nationals and the Regional on an incredible six occasions. Futurian was one of the Top Dogs of all breeds for 1996, and he was BOB at the 1995 Regional and the 1996 Nationals before his untimely death.

It is one of my great disappointments that I never got to see Cachet in the ring because, if I had, I could have decided for myself which of these three 'greats' was, in fact, the greatest. There is no doubt that it would be a very close-run thing, and the debate among breed enthusiasts will rumble on for many years. Elizabeth Esacove told me at the 1997 ABC that her personal opinion was that Futurian had the slight edge.

VANCROFT
Deborah Clark and Marcia Adams
The first Vancroft was purchased as a pet in 1983, soon followed in 1985 by Ch. Gerhards String of Pearls who was to become the kennel's foundation. In 1989, the kennel bred its first litter which contained three Champions, including Ch. Vancroft's Vogue. This bitch was mated to Ch. Misty Valley's Curtain Call and a brindle male from the litter became the kennel's biggest winner to date, the magnificent Ch. Vancroft's Prime Time, who was the ABC Top Twenty winner in 1994. He also has five all-breed Best in Show awards, together with many Groups. In addition, he was Best of Breed at Westminster in 1997 and I was delighted to be in New York to see him take this great win. Prime Time is all Boxer, striking that ideal balance between substance and elegance, and moving so well in profile. It is pleasing to record that he is also breeding on well and he has just become a Sire of Merit.

Over the years, there has been a close association between Vancroft Boxers and the Misty Valley kennels, owned by Brenda and Derek Grice – formerly from England, but now based in Maryland. At present, they are jointly campaigning Ch. Misty Valley Vancroft Beau Derek, a beautiful red and white girl who was the 1997 American Boxer Club Futurity winner. There have been many Vancroft Champions and the kennel has always been keen to look at a range of complementary bloodlines. Deborah and Marcia have been lucky in obtaining some excellent stock from breeders who were willing to part with their best and, because of this, they are not afraid to part with a puppy to help someone else get started.

VIRGO
Virginia and Owen Proctor
Virginia and Owen bought their first Boxer just after their wedding in 1958 but, due to Owen's career in the Air Force and the extensive travelling involved, exhibiting was difficult until his retirement in 1979. An extremely important event in the evolution of the Virgo Boxers was the acquisition of Ch. Merrilane's Lookout in 1988, who was awarded Reserve Winners bitch at the American Boxer Club the day after the Proctors bought her. Since then, the kennel

Ch. Virgo's Market Boomer won more than 150 Best of Breed awards.

has produced many Champions, but the most notable has been Ch. Virgo's Market Boomer. During the three years that Boomer was nationally campaigned, he was always one of the top three Boxers and one of the top twenty dogs in the USA. He won more that 150 Best of Breeds, over 100 Group placements and six all-breed best in shows. So far, he has sired 14 Champions and is a Sire of Merit. One of his daughters, Ch. Virgo's Celebration, was the grand prize winner in the 1995 ABC Futurity Sweepstake and Reserve Winners bitch.

WOODS END
Mrs Jack L. Billhardt
The Billhardts first became Boxer owners in 1958 and they have been breeding and showing since 1965. Over the years, every Boxer which they have kept to show has become a Champion. Their best-known was the American and Canadian Champion, Woods End Million Heir. He was the top owner-bred Boxer during his show career and went on to become a Sire of Merit with 32 Champion children. Another well-known Woods End was Dream Merchant, winner of the American Boxer Club Regional. However, in spite of all the show ring successes, the health and happiness of the dogs has always been the main consideration at Woods End.